Another Gospel

Another Gospel

A Confrontation with Liberation Theology

Paul C. McGlasson

Foreword by Brevard S. Childs

Baker Books

A Division of Baker Book House Co
Grand Rapids, Michigan 49516

© 1994 by Paul C. McGlasson

Published by Baker Books
a division of Baker Book House Company
PO Box 6287, Grand Rapids, Michigan 49516-6287

Printed in the United States of America

Library of Congress Cataloging-in-Publication Data

McGlasson, Paul.
    Another gospel : a confrontation with liberation theology / Paul C. McGlasson.
       p.   cm.
    Includes bibliographical references and index.
    ISBN 0-8010-6315-9
    1. Liberation theology—Controversial literature. 2. Theology, Doctrinal—North America—History—20th century.   I. Title.
    BT83.57.M376   1994
    230'.046—dc20   94-13599

To
Brevard S. Childs
who is worthy of double honor

Contents

Foreword

To suggest that mainline Christianity is in a crisis has become a truism, and it has called forth countless analyses, reports, and proposals. In this hard-hitting, provocative book Paul McGlasson has taken a very different tack. His thesis, which is particularly challenging and a sheer affront to many, is that what is needed is not more dialogue, but decision. In conscious contrast to his two previous academic monographs, McGlasson has here thrown down the gauntlet. The Christian church is faced with a massive theological threat to its gospel that is different in kind from the older frictions between liberals and conservatives. He thus seeks to sound a simple, clarion, clear warning to the church of Jesus Christ for the sake of the gospel.

McGlasson is addressing an audience of ordinary, simple, faithful Christians who have become confused and often quite bewildered by a new language of preaching, teaching, and writing that has found inroads into most mainline denominations. He encompasses this threat within the overarching category of "liberation theology." He writes from the perspective, not of a narrow, intolerant fundamentalism, but rather he seeks to address a threat that has begun to undermine the foundations of the basic confessional tradition of the universal church of Jesus Christ, encompassing the theological faith of both Protestants and Catholics, and grounded on both the ancient and modern creeds of our faith.

The heart of the confrontation lies in his claim that an ideology has sought to replace—the mode word is "reinterpret"—the traditional, evangelical message of the gospel that sees therein an act of sheer grace on the part of God in Jesus Christ effecting salvation to those who receive this divine gift in faith (Rom. 1:17). Through the Holy Spirit God brought forth a new creation according to the image of the risen Lord by overcoming the powers of sin and evil on the cross.

In striking contrast we are now being told that the preaching of Jesus of the kingdom of God had as its goal the tearing down of all forms of social hierarchy and of building an egalitarian society. Salvation has been reinterpreted as forms of human liberation from all kinds of hierarchy, patriarchy, and cultural oppression. The church is now viewed as an extension of Christ's redemptive ministry through its acts of social activism against societal, political, and economic evils, and has become a partner in realizing the divine intent for the world. As a result, Jesus is portrayed as the leader of egalitarian justice and peace movements throughout the world, and the kingdom of God has been turned into a modern egalitarian utopia of the Enlightenment with its goal of self-fulfillment. One hears nothing of atonement, of justification from sin, of the call of faith, of walking in the Spirit, and of the eschatological hope of Christ's final triumphant victory over sin and death. For this reason McGlasson denounces this teaching, however nuanced in its various formulations, as false doctrine.

The author then seeks to show how each of the crucial doctrines of the faith has been distorted by liberation theology. God is no longer the divine Person, one God in three modes, whom the church confessed in its doctrine of the Trinity. Rather, God is known through endless symbols of human experience, but without a named identity. Scripture is not the living voice of God continuing to provide an unswerving source of truth and guidance, but rather a loose composition of metaphors without any determinate meaning, which remains inert until human imagination gives the symbols a function. By means of an appeal to "contextualization" the Bible is robbed of its authority for faith and practice, and every text is turned on its head as a warrant for private agenda. Finally, faith becomes a symbol of martyrdom to the cause of partnership toward some temporal end. In a word, what is being "empowered" is simply the old sinful, unredeemed human self. The New Testament's promise of the fruits of the Spirit, and the joyful confession of true freedom in Christ (Rom. 8), have been lost in the search for personal fulfillment and human worth.

It is a fundamental misreading of McGlasson's book to see it as an arrogant exercise in the naming of heretics. Rather, this powerful confrontation turns on the central questions of basic theological substance. *Positions* are judged heretical in the light of Scripture and according to the universal confessions of the church throughout the ages. McGlasson is fully aware of the crucial distinction, clearly articulated in the creeds, that the naming of heretics remains the task of the corporate body of the church, not of an individual. McGlasson is writing polemical theology, but it is not sectarian. Indeed, it is just the opposite in its challenging of a growing number of theologians who claim to speak for the church while denying the very source of its true universal identity.

History bears continual testimony to certain moments in the life of the church that proved crucial to its very existence. In his letter to the Galatians Paul staked the truth of the whole gospel on the seemingly picayune controversy over table fellowship. Indeed, it is usually from within the church, from the pious, well-meaning theologians like Arius, Sabellius, and Pelagius, that heresy arose. Moreover, Athanasius,

Augustine, Luther, and Calvin were all vilified for sounding the alarm. It would be foolhardy to predict the response to McGlasson's challenge. Surely some will be deeply offended. But many will be strengthened and given new resolve for the sake of Christ. Is not such a defense of the gospel in these decisive days our God-given duty and worthy of the watchman's role? Finally, a word of appreciation to the publisher of Paul McGlasson's controversial book is in order. At a time in which most of the denominational presses have felt forced to conform to mode theology, or have been cowed by the pressures of political and religious "correctness," it is encouraging still to discover evidence of courage, independence, and resoluteness.

BREVARD S. CHILDS
Sterling Professor of Divinity
Yale University

Preface

Christian theology, if it is worthy of the name, must in times of crisis be concerned with aiding the church in defending the parameters of the faith, outside of which the gospel is not rightly preached. In performing this task, theology must rely upon the canonical authority of Holy Scripture alone. I wish to express my esteem and gratitude for the brilliant work of Brevard S. Childs, whose work on Scripture as canon is of inestimable value.

I am grateful to my wife Peggy, for her wonderful support and advice; and to my mother and father, for their support and encouragement. I wish to express my special thanks to Baker Book House for publishing this volume, and to Allan Fisher, Jim Weaver, and Maria E. denBoer.

The present volume is written at a time of enormous crisis in the church, which has been ravaged by the false prophets of so-called liberation theology. And yet, in the midst of severe crisis, I acknowledge with thanksgiving and praise the gracious hand of the Lord.

Introduction

Circumstances of the Present Work

There is a time to plant, and a time to pluck up; this is a time to pluck up. There is a time to mourn, and a time to dance; this is a time to mourn. There is a time to rend, and a time to sew; this is a time to rend. There is a time to keep silence, and a time to speak; this is a time to speak (cf. Eccl. 3:1–8).

I write the present work with one aim in mind: to lay a charge at the feet of a widespread segment of American Christianity, particularly in seminary education, of defection from the gospel of Jesus Christ. These are hard words, and they will be followed in this book by further still.

I who make this charge have no reputation, and so I do not base my charge upon repute. Neither do I have ecclesiastical standing or influence of note, and so I do not base my charge upon influence. I write as a minister of the Word of God, and it is upon this basis alone that I make my charge. If the charge I make does not accord with Holy Scripture, I beg the reader to dismiss it at once as baseless. But if it does accord with Holy Scripture, I exhort the reader not to fear, but to have courage—"for God did not give us a spirit of timidity but a spirit of power and love and self-control" (2 Tim. 1:7).

Against whom do I make the charge? Against those who espouse the views and tactics of the so-called liberation theology. Indeed, one could for a time wonder: there are liberation theologians, and there are liberation theologians. Can one cast one's net so broadly? Must one not distinguish the various movements, and voices within the movements, and assess each case by case? Perhaps for a time; but now is not that time. I referred above to the views *and* the tactics, because liberation theology is no longer a view alone, offered for thoughtful consideration and debate in the churches; it has rather become a party, a movement, which through "force and insincere practices" (Barmen Declaration) has permeated the life of the church, and perverted and twisted the church's mission, its message, and its good order.

Who are the liberation theologians? We shall consider some historical background below; there are feminist liberation theologies, black liberation theologies, Hispanic liberation theologies, neoorthodox liberation theologies, evangelical liberation theologies, Roman Catholic liberation theologies. Liberation theology is taught in virtually every seminary in mainline Christianity in North America. And more, it threatens to eclipse the preaching of the Word from the pulpits of the American churches. But "the word of God is not fettered" (2 Tim. 2:9).

In less than three decades, liberation theology has swept across the landscape of theological education. And it is now the street-talk of large segments of the local church. It has recently been called the "new reformation" within American Christianity. And we are often told that we must not stand in the way of the new reformation, must not miss the work of the Spirit. But the sword of the Spirit of God is the Word of God (Eph. 6:17); and the enemy of the Spirit of truth is the spirit of error (1 John 4:1–6). We are commanded to test the spirits, to see whether they are of God; and we are given a sure rule of faith in Holy Scripture by which we may know whether they are of God or of the spirit of Antichrist.

The claim to be made in the present work, in light of Holy Scripture alone as the sure rule of faith in the church of Jesus Christ, is that liberation theology is a lie. "Not that there is another gospel, but there are some who trouble you and want to pervert the gospel of Christ" (Gal. 1:7). If it is not the gospel of Jesus Christ, what is the so-called liberation theology? It is another gospel, an ideology cast up by the resources of our time in its agonizing alienation from the love of God in Jesus Christ. It is many -isms, but fundamentally one -ism: egalitarianism. The reign of God, we are told, is the coming world in which all human life is in partnership. And the great enemy of the reign of God is hierarchical power. Human beings are to build partnership with one another, breaking down the oppressive structures of power that characterize the world. Human beings have been taught true partnership with God, casting aside the distorted patriarchal view of God in the Bible. Human beings are to build partnership with nature, overcoming the false alienation from nature resulting from patriarchal dominance. This, we are told, is what Jesus taught, and what he gave his life to inaugurate.

This, I submit, is not what Jesus taught, nor is it what he gave his life for. According to Holy Scripture, such views are lies; they pervert the gospel and profane the life, death, and resurrection of our Lord and Savior. We are often told by the so-called liberation theologians that each of us comes to Scripture with our own experience and context; and no doubt I would be told that my rejection of these views comes from my experience and context. I certainly do not deny my own time-conditionality. Nor do I deny that on some issues good Christian folk rightly disagree concerning the interpretation of Scripture. But according to Scripture itself, on some issues the gospel itself is at stake. On some issues, there is not interpretation, only yes or no. On some issues there is not useful dialogue, only decision. It is the authority of the Word alone that tells us where we face these issues. And it is the authority of the Word alone—what other authority am I exercising?—to which I here appeal. If I am right, then there can be only one conclusion: so-called liberation theology is a heresy that threatens the unity of the church. Those who teach it ought not to be hired; those who preach it ought not to be listened to; those who by tactics and insincere practices seek to force it on the church ought to be exposed. To whom do I make such an appeal? I appeal to the people of God in the mainline churches in North America. I write to those who confess Jesus Christ as Lord and Savior, to encourage you to hold fast that confession in the face of the threat of liberation theology.

Historical Background

The historical background and development of liberation theology have been rehearsed in countless books and articles, and is too well known to require full treatment here. The names and dates are well known—how it emerged from the turbulent era of the late 1960s, arising in the context of European political thought, Latin American liberation movements, the black consciousness movement, and the feminist movement. One thinks immediately of the names of Gustavo Gutiérrez, James Cone, Mary Daly, Rosemary Ruether, and countless others.

But here we must dig deeper. By the 1970s and 1980s, liberation theology was clearly emerging as the theological consensus for the times. What was the secret of its success? On the surface, there was a "prophetic" critique of culture, government, technology, and so forth, and in particular all forms of human "hierarchy." Was this the final end of the older cultural Christianity of liberalism, with its easy correlation of Christianity and culture? It is here that we discern the optical illusion of liberation theology. For the standard of its critique is not God's revealed will in his Word, but the political-cultural agenda of the left. That is to say, it has rejected an easy cultural Christianity, only to introduce an easy countercultural Christianity. But from the standpoint of the Word, they are identical; the difference is merely in the cultural resources that are used. Where once the resources of high culture were used, now the resources of counterculture are used. Where once we heard "heteronomy" denounced, now we hear "hierarchy" denounced. Where once we heard of "correlation," now we hear of "partnership." Where once we heard from Enlightenment high culture, "*sapere aude!*" ("dare to think!"), now we hear from counterculture, "I am somebody!" Liberation theology is liberalism for the "new generation."

But we must press the issue a step further. Why is it that liberation theology was able so swiftly to sweep across theological education, with a few notable exceptions, almost unopposed? Indeed, must we not look even closer at its historical origin and growth, if we are truly to understand its success?

Why was it so able to capture the imagination of so many in the black church? The black consciousness movement, on the one hand, is a scarcely disguised attempt to co-opt the Christian church for an ideological agenda. But what about the civil rights movement? Despite the obvious good work of the movement as a reform movement in American politics, was it not from the beginning burdened by an ideological dimension that profoundly contradicts Holy Scripture? Was it not Dr. Martin Luther King, Jr., who sought to combine an unequal alliance between the gospel of Jesus Christ and the ideological agenda of the Enlightenment? It is indeed fortunate that the roots of the faith have sunk very deep in the black church, so that despite those who would prey upon it for ideological purposes, it continues to remain resilient.

And why was it so able to arrest the attention of theologians and laity in the Roman Catholic Church? Was it not long the custom in Roman Catholic theology to argue for natural theology, an access to the reality of God apart from

God's revelation in Jesus Christ as he is attested for us in Holy
Scripture? But perhaps most importantly in North American Christianity, where were the theologians of the Reformation,
grounded in Holy Scripture as the Word of God? When one
thinks back over the past three decades, it is agonizingly
clear that a whole generation of biblical and systematic theologians, in particular supposedly Reformed theologians,
have not only not protested, but have indeed joined the
crowd, with ever-increasing volume. Liberation theology is
often disguised by a veneer of biblical authority, and perhaps in some there lurks beneath this veneer the memory
of an almost forgotten faith. But from a whole generation of
theologians and biblical scholars from whom one should
have expected protest, has come acquiescence.

And here we must dig deeper still. For so many of the
previous generation had read Karl Barth, and therefore
should have known better. But must we not question Barth
himself, who otherwise did so much to reform the church
by the Word of God? Was it not Barth who confessed the faith
in opposition to the political right, but who refused to do so
in opposition to the political left? Was it not Barth who
sought to combine the humiliation and exaltation of Jesus
Christ into two movements of his earthly life, thus distorting the witness of Scripture that first he suffered and then
he was exalted? Was it not Barth who returned to the theme
of natural theology? Was it not Barth who at least was
ambiguous late in his life on the question of the scandal of
particularity, that there is no salvation outside of Jesus
Christ? Was it not Barth who, though he wrote so wonder-
fully on the free and sovereign grace of our Redeemer, wrote
so little on the response of faith and the life of the Christian?
Was it not Barth who so fused incarnation and revelation,
as to minimize the hiddenness of the gospel in its reality,
thus again diminishing the need for the response of faith?
These questions of Barth come only painfully to one who

has learned so much from him. Nevertheless, is it not significant that so many students and readers of Barth have not swum against the stream, as he once so courageously did? And what of preaching in the churches of mainline Christianity in North America? It is as if only the pastors and theologians fail to see just how far we have fallen away from preaching the Word of God based on Holy Scripture alone as our norm. It is a shock, indeed a disgrace, to discover that many of our newer pastors have never been exposed to anything else but the so-called liberation theology. Truths that the faithful in the church know by heart in the deepest recesses of their being have, by older pastors and theologians, been so maligned and ridiculed that some now being trained are unaware that it is the faith itself that is being neglected and forgotten.

And while liberation theology has not been the only chapter in theology in the past three decades, what other option has not either been co-opted into the movement, or murmured off to the side about the decline of the church, but without saying no to liberation theology when it is time to say no? Where are the narrative theologians? Where are the various ecclesiological models of doctrine and Scripture and ethics? Where are the neoevangelical theologians?

Is there no truth whatsoever in liberation theology? As in other heresies, there is in liberation theology the distant echo of a biblical truth: the profound biblical witness to God's special embrace of and invitation to the poor, the outcast, the marginalized. As Paul testifies: "For consider your call, brethren; not many of you were wise according to worldly standards, not many were powerful, not many were of noble birth" (1 Cor. 1:26). But, as in other heresies, the truth is put into a context foreign to the rule of faith in Holy Scripture, in this case the context of egalitarian ideology. And so the resulting theology is a monstrous maligning of the good confession of the Christian: "Let him who boasts, boast of the Lord" (1 Cor. 1:31b). Liberation theology is another gospel. That is the claim I shall now argue. I shall argue it in the light of one hermeneutical reality: that Jesus Christ is not dead, but risen, and speaks for himself in his Word by his Spirit, calling for the obedience of faith.

1

Jesus Christ

The Scandal of Particularity

There is talk of Jesus Christ in liberation theology, but it is not the gospel that is being proclaimed. Jesus of Nazareth, we are told, was God's special representative, God's chosen one, who proclaimed and lived the radically new reign of God. Continuing in the line of the prophetic tradition of Israel, Jesus overturned all forms of human hierarchy, thus both bearing witness to and inaugurating in his lifetime the reign of God. His preaching and his deeds called forth severe opposition, especially among the hierarchical leaders of the time, who consequently put him to death on a Roman cross. But what he inaugurated continues in the work of his disciples, who seek to build the kingdom for which he himself gave his life.

This, I submit, is false doctrine. We shall dig more deeply theologically in a moment, but we begin with the clearest indication of heresy, and that is the denial of the scandal of particularity. With unambiguous clarity, Scripture professes that there is no salvation outside of Jesus Christ. "And there is salvation in no one else, for there is no other name under heaven given among men by which we must be saved" (Acts 4:12) is the scandal of the apostolic kerygma, which faith knows to be the power of God unto salvation, but over which unbelief stumbles. Jesus himself declares to us: "I am the way, and the truth, and the life; no one comes to the Father, but by me" (John 14:6). And it is stated in deepest fear and trembling that it is the spirit of Antichrist that denies that Jesus Christ is the Son of God (1 John 2:18–25).

We hear many impressive things said of Jesus among liberation theologians. But what we hear less and less, if at all, is the Christian confession that Jesus Christ is the Son of God. And what we hear not at all, but often expressly denied, is the Christian confession that there is no salvation outside of Jesus Christ. There is a great deal of theological doublespeak that masks and legitimates the heresy. We hear of multicultural globalism, ecumenicity, and interfaith dialogue; we hear of postmodern limits to human experience and of the hermeneutics of suspicion; we hear trumpet blasts against neotribalism and a joyful affirmation of pluralism. But what lies behind the strange theological doublespeak is a vast movement of theology and preaching that denies the gospel, by denying, or failing to affirm, the scandal of particularity. Where Jesus Christ is not confessed as God's one act of salvation for the world, there is not the gospel, but the Antichrist.

Messianism as Ideology

If it is not the Jesus Christ of the gospel who is being professed, what is being professed? Jesus, we are told, was the one who preached the reign of God, which is the tearing down of hierarchy and the building of an egalitarian society. Where is this in Holy Scripture? It is not there. The ethics of the kingdom of God as Jesus proclaimed it does not point in this direction. Instead, what is being described as the "reign of God" is the modern egalitarian ideology of the Enlightenment, which is then attached to the figure of Jesus. The result is that Jesus becomes the architect of a movement, the leader of a cause, the so-called Jesus movement, which is the cause of egalitarian justice and peace throughout the world. Now, it is obvious enough that Jesus is not the only person ever to proclaim and live by this creed; he may indeed have been God's special representative, and hence in that sense divine, but there are other valid ways to be captured by the "vision" of the coming reign of God on earth and the human challenge to build it. And so Jesus is one avenue among others to God's reign on earth.

Because of the nature of egalitarian ideology, each group within liberation theology has to have its own version of the Jesus of the reign of God. And so there are feminist Christologies, and black Christologies, and native American Christologies, and Hispanic Christologies, and so forth. And while there are some differences, each claims to find in Jesus the one who will empower them to full partnership in the coming reign of God.

What we are hearing about Jesus from liberation theologians is not Jesus Christ himself as he is attested for us in Holy Scripture; what we are hearing about is a "Jesus" who functions much like a leader in the civil rights movement. The theological doublespeak is rather thick; but serious reflection on what is being said ultimately resolves itself into a figure more or less equivalent to Martin Luther King. Martin Kaehler, in his *The So-Called Historical Jesus and the Historic-Biblical Christ,* reached the same conclusion a century ago concerning the Protestant liberal Jesus: the Protestant liberal version of Jesus was an ideological projection of the spirit of the age. And the problem is much the same; where Scripture alone is not the one rule of faith in the church, the door is wide open for ideologies of the age to come pouring in. Indeed, it is not altogether clear that it is not in fact the same ideology that Kaehler exposed! It is not now high-culture liberalism that is perverting the gospel; but is it not simply multicultural liberalism? And doesn't the Jesus who emerges bear striking resemblance to the older view? Is it no accident that the "kingdom of God," properly retooled to meet the needs of a multicultural audience, is again the key to the identity of Jesus, as it was for liberalism? Did not King himself rely heavily upon the resources of modernity—recall his use of Thoreau—for the construction of his movement?

Still, whether it is a repetition of the older liberal lives of Jesus, or a newer and different form, the fact remains that the "Jesus" of liberation theology is not the Jesus Christ of Holy Scripture. Liberation theologians will of course deny this; but the rule of faith to determine the truth of their claim is clear and dependable in Holy Scripture: Are they professing that there is no salvation outside of Jesus Christ? If not, they are not professing Jesus Christ; and "no one who denies the Son has the Father" (1 John 2:23).

It is important to note at this point that the problem does not lie in the historical-critical method, but in the ideological use of the method. The scandal of particularity is affirmed clearly and boldly in the apostolic kerygma; and yet it is denied by the pluralism of liberation theology. What accounts for the discrepancy? How is it that the text of Holy Scripture can make a clear christological affirmation that is then expressly denied? The problem does not lie in the method. The historical-critical method itself simply clarifies what the New Testament openly declares about faith: the faith of the Christian church is not built on a supposedly historical access to a supposedly reconstructed historical Jesus. Rather, the faith of the church is grounded in the risen Lord, who shows us the identity of his earthly life in his Word by his Spirit. "But when the Counselor comes, whom I shall send to you from the Father, even the Spirit of truth, who proceeds from the Father, he will bear witness to me" (John 15:26). This is the "Spirit of truth, whom the world cannot receive" (John 14:17), but which engenders the response of faith. Because it is based on the ideological illusion of a historical access to the "historical Jesus," liberation theology contradicts the witness of Scripture itself, seeking to bypass, as it were, the Spirit, the Word, and faith. But that is to bypass Jesus Christ himself.

Theologia gloriae

Our thesis for the present work is that liberation theology is a heresy; it is false witness to Jesus Christ. We are also concerned to inquire, however, how it could be that virtually a generation of biblical scholars and theologians, especially in Reformed circles in North America, could either stand idly by or be actively engaged in the propagation of liberation theology. We have argued that the civil rights movement contributed the egalitarian ideology that maligned the witness of the gospel. But why is it that this ideology could so quickly, and so thoroughly, infest the learned community of theology in North America?

Here I must turn to the figure of Karl Barth. Perhaps this comes as a surprise. After all, who could have been more courageous in standing up against false ideology in the church? And indeed it is so. Who could have been more conspicuous in the affirmation of Jesus Christ in theology? And indeed it is so. And yet again we must wrestle with the question, why it is that in circles of Barth's influence in North America the ideology of egalitarianism so quickly and so deeply spread? Why was it, for example, that in the 1967 Confession of the Presbyterian Church, the ideology of egalitarianism, replete with the familiar buzz-words of the social action gospel, became enshrined in the confessional literature of that denomination? How could it be that a single denomination could have in its book of confessions a powerful document like the Barmen Declaration, exposing and

opposing, often to the death of its adherents (and to the loss
of Barth's employment in Germany) the ideology of the right,
and yet also the Confession of 1967, virtually adopting the
ideology of the left as the gospel—the very error of the German Christians?
Future historians will need to unravel the development
with more historical distance, but for the present I must
return to the theological witness of Barth. We begin with the
recognition that Barth himself came late in life to deny the
scandal of particularity, in his work *Evangelical Theology:
An Introduction* (in particular, in lecture 1). We have already
seen that here Scripture speaks with clarity, and the Christian church has always recognized that this is a line beyond
which is not the gospel of Jesus Christ. And indeed, anyone
who has read the *Church Dogmatics* and is familiar with the
basic course of Barth's theological work, will know that he
too often spoke boldly of the scandal of particularity. This
is all the more reason to be troubled by this unfortunate turn
in his later thinking.

But surely it was not so long ago in the churches in North
America that salvation in Jesus Christ alone was proclaimed
joyfully and reverently? Again, we must stand back, astonished and bewildered that so much could be lost so quickly.
Where, we continue to ask, were those who know from Scripture the clear rule of faith, and yet hide or even openly deny
it? Indeed, it is most common now, as everyone knows, to
hear from theologians and biblical scholars in the Reformed
world even open ridicule of the scandal of particularity.
Under the strange theological doublespeak of the times,
there is ridicule—fundamentalists!—of those who hold fast
the good confession of the faith. These are deceivers!

But we must return to Barth, again seeking to discern why
so many under his influence could come to confuse the
gospel with a victorious political ideology on the left. We
suggest, in continuing our reflections, that features of Barth's
own Christology fell short of the witness of Scripture—in

particular, his attempt to fuse humiliation and exaltation into two movements of the incarnate One, rather than as a clear temporal progression. Scripture professes that Christ humbled himself, taking the form of a servant, being born in the likeness of men, suffering for our sins on the cross. And therefore God highly exalted him, bestowing on him the name which is above every name (Phil. 2:1–11). The affirmation of the scandal of particularity is grounded in the witness that Christ was first humbled, then God exalted him. This is what the structure of Barth's Christology, for all its brilliant detail, overlooks.

But does not the very One who suffered and died for the sins of the world, whom God highly exalted above every name, does not Jesus Christ himself command us in his Word to suffer in obedience to his will? Does not liberation theology despise and reject the command of the Lord to suffer, seeking instead exaltation now without suffering first? To be sure, we are not to *seek* suffering: "A prudent man sees danger and hides himself; but the simple go on, and suffer for it" (Prov. 22:3). But the gospel calls us to attachment to Jesus Christ in such a way as to set us apart from the ideologies of the world, on the left and the right; it proclaims that the suffering of unjust abuse is willingly to be endured for the sake of him who died for the sins of the world. Why? Because he is worthy, who did not despise us or hate us, but who loved us, even unto death on a cross for our sins.

I must return to Barth. Did he not so fuse incarnation and revelation throughout the *Church Dogmatics,* as though the incarnation itself were the revelation, apart from the response of faith? Scripture boldly professes the mystery of the incarnate One, in whom all the fullness of God dwelt bodily. And yet, in the witness of Scripture, one could be standing right in front of him in his earthly life, and not know his identity. Barth's biblical exegesis in particular continually rides roughshod over the clear sense of the text. Barth understands the rich young ruler, for example, to be one who acknowledges the kingly authority of Jesus. And yet the whole point of the text turns on Jesus' exposing of the sin of the rich young ruler, his willful rejection of God's good will, which Jesus himself annunciates. In other words, Barth consistently distorts, both exegetically and dogmatically, the basic mystery of the incarnation: that Jesus of Nazareth was the Son of God incarnate, but in concealment from unbelief.

And so again we are dismayed, though no longer as surprised, that a generation of Reformed theologians and biblical scholars could talk loudly and confidently about the divine identity of Jesus Christ, only to lose that identity in an ever-increasing volume of ideological harangue. But the subject matter itself does not stand idly by. To those who would combine the witness to Christ with the ideologies of the world, Jesus himself says: "I know your works: you are neither cold nor hot. Would that you were cold or hot! So, because you are lukewarm, and neither cold nor hot, I will spew you out of my mouth" (Rev. 3:15–16). These are hard words, but they come with a promise: "Those whom I love, I reprove and chasten; so be zealous and repent. Behold, I stand at the door and knock; if any one hears my voice and opens the door, I will come in to him and eat with him, and he with me. He who conquers, I will grant him to sit with me on my throne, as I myself conquered and sat down with my Father on his throne. He who has an ear, let him hear what the Spirit says to the churches" (Rev. 3:19–20).

Fides ex auditu

The church must recover in its theology and preaching the basic confession of faith itself: that Jesus Christ is not dead, but risen, and speaks for himself in his Word by the Holy Spirit, calling forth the response of faith. This means, on the one hand, that any attempt of the church to enter into partnership with Jesus concerning his identity will end in utter disaster. He alone addresses us in sovereign freedom in his Word, calling not for partnership but for the obedience of faith. But this means, on the other hand, that attempts to unconceal his true identity apart from the response of faith will likewise end in disaster. He alone speaks for himself in his Word by his Spirit; he alone opens hearts and minds to know and believe in him. We must, as Luther put it, preach and pray. We must preach Christ crucified and risen for the salvation of the world, calling for the obedience of faith, and pray for God to use our witness according to his gracious purpose. And we must always look to ourselves, "lest after preaching to others I myself should be disqualified" (1 Cor. 9:27)

2

Salvation

Sola gratia

We are told by the liberation theologians and preachers that Jesus saves people by empowering them. Jesus sides with the poor and the oppressed, giving them worth and dignity. And in Jesus' preaching there goes forth to his disciples the recognition of God's mission in the world: to be about the task of building the kingdom that Jesus proclaimed and for which he died.

We have argued that the Jesus professed by liberation theologians is not Jesus Christ as he is attested for us in Scripture alone, and is therefore not Jesus Christ. We now continue our critique by stating that the salvation that is proclaimed among liberation theologians is not the salvation offered by the gospel.

The clearest indication of this is the raging Pelagianism of liberation theologians and preachers. Above all else, we are told, it is up to us to build the kingdom; we are in partnership with God in the carrying out of God's mission in the world. This is not the view of Scripture; indeed, it is contradicted by the clear testimony of the gospel.

In a gross distortion of the witness of the Old Testament, the concept of the covenant is often appealed to in this context, as if the covenant of the people of Israel were a kind of pact, or joint venture for liberation, between Israel and God. A whole mythology of exodus has been created around this twisted view, as if the exodus were an empowerment of the people of Israel to their own historical agency.

What does Scripture say?

> For you are a people holy to the LORD your God; the LORD your God has chosen you to be a people for his own possession, out of all the peoples that are on the face of the earth. It was not because you were more in number than any other people that the LORD set his love upon you and chose you, for you were the fewest of all peoples; but it is because the LORD loves you, and is keeping the oath which he swore to your fathers, that the LORD has brought you out with a mighty hand, and redeemed you from the house of bondage, from the hand of Pharaoh, king of Egypt. Know therefore that the LORD your God is God, the faithful God who keeps covenant and steadfast love with those who love him and keep his commandments, to a thousand generations, and requites to their face those who hate him, by destroying them; he will not be slack with him who hates him, he will requite him to his face. You shall therefore be careful to do the commandment, and the statutes, and the ordinances, which I command you this day. (Deut. 7:6–11)

The great themes of the witness of the Old Testament to salvation—the election of God based on the unfathomable mystery of his love, the sovereign act of God in redeeming Israel from bondage, the gracious binding of the people of

God into a covenant calling for the response of obedience—
are missing entirely from the mythology of exodus among
liberation theologians and preachers. Indeed, the very errors
of sinful Israel are made again and again by this "community." Did God redeem Israel to historical agency? Was it not
precisely this conviction that led Israel to utter apostasy in
the building of the golden calf—the first "people's theology"?
Did God enter into "partnership" with Israel, calling forth a
devout "spirituality" celebrating the partnership? Did he not
say to the "spiritual" people of "liberated" Israel: "If I were
hungry, I would not tell you; for the world and all that is in
it is mine. Do I eat the flesh of bulls, or drink the blood of
goats? Offer to God a sacrifice of thanksgiving, and pay your
vows to the Most High; and call upon me in the day of trouble; I will deliver you, and you shall glorify me" (Ps. 50:12–15)?
Did he not say in scorn to the "empowered" people of "the
exodus community": "'Are you not like the Ethiopians to me,
O people of Israel?' says the LORD. 'Did I not bring up Israel
from the land of Egypt, and the Philistines from Caphtor and
the Syrians from Kir? Behold, the eyes of the Lord GOD are
upon the sinful kingdom, and I will destroy it from the surface of the ground; except that I will not utterly destroy the
house of Jacob,' says the LORD" (Amos 9:7–8)?

We are perhaps astonished at the utter failure of the liberation theologians and preachers to understand the basic
witness of the Old Testament. And yet we are not so astonished. For we remember that the church of Jesus Christ confesses that only Jesus Christ himself, by his Spirit, can open
our minds to understand the witness of the Old Testament
to the one reality of salvation in him (Luke 24:27).

And matters are no different when we consider the New
Testament. Where is "empowerment"? Where is "building
the kingdom of God"? Where is "partnership with God"?
Instead we hear: "But now the righteousness of God has
been manifested apart from law, although the law and the
prophets bear witness to it, the righteousness of God

through faith in Jesus Christ for all who believe. For there is no distinction; since all have sinned and fall short of the glory of God, they are justified by his grace as a gift, through the redemption which is in Christ Jesus, whom God put forward as an expiation by his blood, to be received by faith. This was to show God's righteousness, because in his divine forbearance he had passed over former sins; it was to prove at the present time that he himself is righteous and that he justifies him who has faith in Jesus" (Rom. 3:21–26). We hear that God alone has done what we could not do, sending his son to die as a sacrifice for our sins; not based on our worth or merit, but out of the overwhelming reality of his love. Of a God who freely gives his Spirit, engendering the response of faith and rendering us a new creation in Christ Jesus.

In both Testaments, salvation is by grace alone from beginning to end. Liberation theology and preaching twist and distort and ultimately deny the gospel as it is attested in both Testaments of Holy Scripture. We must also point out the typical shape of the distortion: first appeal is made to a mythology of exodus and covenant-partnership with the "exodus community"; then, appeal is made to the proclamation of Jesus concerning the kingdom of God, though here the appeal is very loose and usually amounts to a few select verses or broad themes from the historically reconstructed "Jesus movement." And yet, this flies right in the face of the kerygma of the early church, which did not use the exodus as the basis for its witness, which denied access to the reality of the Old Testament witness apart from Jesus Christ himself, and which spoke not a single word, ever, about human building of the kingdom.

Salvation by Worth

We hear a great deal about the "kingdom of God" from teachers and preachers of liberation theology (though increasingly referred to as "the reign of God" so as not to offend feminist sensibilities). What exactly does this mean?

The kingdom of God, we are told, is a world in which the intrinsic worth of everyone will be affirmed—a world without class, without gender dualism, without hierarchy of any kind. Liberation (which is the word used for salvation among liberation theologians) means God's empowerment to self-fulfillment. It means the removal of restraints on my right to self-fulfillment, be those restraints social, moral, political, or religious. Moreover, salvation as liberation means that God is particularly concerned to remove the restraints on the self-fulfillment of the marginalized and powerless. God saves by giving power to the powerless, thus empowering them to claim and act upon the fundamental human right of personal and historical agency.

This is, of course, the basic ideology of the civil rights movement in the 1960s, with its own clear antecedents in the Enlightenment. In a generation it has effectively insinuated itself into the Christian community, leading astray wherever it goes; but this is not the gospel of Jesus Christ. It was the teaching of Dr. Martin Luther King, Jr.; it is not the gospel of Jesus Christ.

Have we forgotten everything? Men and women, black and white, once pointed to Jesus Christ and said, "He is everything!"; for God has made him "our wisdom, our righteousness and sanctification and redemption" (1 Cor. 1:30). But now we hear, "I am somebody!" This is not a subtle difference; this is not a different "interpretation" based on a different "context" of experience, to use the strange double-speak of the liberation theologians. This is a fundamental rejection of the grace of God. It is the old Adam shaking his fist at his Creator, refusing to be blessed by him and refusing to obey him. It is the old Adam no longer honoring God as God or giving him thanks. It is the rebellious people of Israel, murmuring in the wilderness against the One who had redeemed them and had given them the promise, insisting, in the deepest folly of human sin and pride, on their rights over and against God, rather than trusting and obeying the One who had redeemed them freely by his mercy. And here I must address a word—who am I to do so?—to my black brothers and sisters. For here, too, we are often hearing strange words, where once we heard the gospel. Can it be that you, too, have forgotten? For how utterly different was the liturgical and theological witness of the black church during and after the emancipation from slavery on the one hand, and the civil rights movement on the other. Then we heard the confession: yes, we too are sinners, we too have fallen short of God's glory; but thanks be to God for his mercy in Jesus Christ! He died for all! But for a generation we have heard nothing but the blame and anger of every ideology: I am somebody! And you have deprived me of my rights to be that somebody! Then we heard the wisdom of the gospel, which knew the false allure of status and wealth and privilege; now we hear the folly of idolatry, rejecting the free gift of God for the sake of self-fulfillment; then we heard the prayer for deliverance—and thanks be to God that prayer was answered; now we hear nothing but murmuring in the wilderness. Now we hear, in disgusting human arrogance, that the "Balm in Gilead" was found in the north. Have you forgotten—but who am I to ask—our greatest treasure?

We hear from the liberation theologians and preachers that God affirms our worth, where the hierarchical structures of society deny it. Our worth is thus based on our power, and so the God who affirms our worth also acts to empower us. Again, the doublespeak is rather thick: one hears of "psychic wholeness," of the "self grounded in community," or of the "healing of the self"; but behind it all lies the gospel of self-fulfillment. How utterly graceless! Have we forgotten everything? That God does not love us based on our worth, or our achievements, but freely by his grace and mercy? That *I* have sinned—Romans 7—and am accountable to God for my sin, though completely unable to free myself from its guilt and power? That despite my sin,

God does not hate or despise me, but sent his Son to bear the penalty of my sin on the cross, simply because God loves me and wants to be with me? The kingdom of God as it is preached and taught by liberation theologians is not the kingdom of God proclaimed by Jesus Christ. It is not the kingdom that I receive with the gratitude and vulnerability of a child (Matt. 18:1–4), but the kingdom that I snatch from God's own hand. It is not the kingdom that I must be born again in order to see (John 3:3), but the kingdom that is based on self-declared worth. It is messianism without the one true Messiah, and therefore the kingdom of the evil one (Matt. 4:8–10).

Covenant-Partnership

But where were all the Reformed theologians and biblical scholars? Again, we must press the case that the obvious perversion of the gospel that comes from the egalitarian ideology of the 1960s is only the surface of the story. Where once the Confessing Church in Germany said no to the ideology on the political right, now, on similar soil in North America, the Presbyterian Church not only did not say no, but simply adopted the ideology of the political left. How had Confessing Christians come to be just like the German Christians under Hitler?

Again, we must return to the theology of Karl Barth. For it was in the later volumes of the *Church Dogmatics* that Barth began to speak of a covenant-partnership between God and humanity. And, according to Barth, this covenant-partnership is the basis for understanding God's reconciliation of the world in Jesus Christ. But is this not a complete reversal of the witness of Scripture? We do not come to the person of Jesus Christ armed with our own concepts of salvation, even supposedly drawn from the Old Testament, then to affirm that Jesus meets our determination. Rather, it is the person and work of Jesus Christ himself who defines for us, in sovereign freedom, the reality of the free gift of salvation. Barth has reversed the relation between the Messiah and the salvation that he offers. We have already seen its dreadful effect on Barth's ability to confess the identity of the Messiah; now we must observe the effect it has on his ability to describe the salvation that Christ offers.

For Barth, Scripture is to be read as a *Bundesgeschichte*, a history of the covenant between God and humanity. But where in Scripture could Barth find any support whatsoever for calling it a partnership? Indeed from dozens of texts in Barth's work one could cite countless references to the sovereign freedom of God's grace in the salvation of the creature. What one finds less attention to is the necessary response of the creature to God's almighty act of salvation. There is in Scripture a paradox of the indicative and the imperative; on the one hand, the grace of God is totally free, and on the other hand, the gospel calls for a human response as a condition for receiving it, with the confession that the response itself is part of the free gift of grace. Without attention to the response of faith, the paradox is unraveled; the result is a "covenant-partnership" that subverts both the free grace and, as we shall see, the human response.

Karl Barth subvert free grace? But remember in the later volumes of the *Dogmatics* how Barth, in astonishingly cavalier fashion, removes justification by faith alone from the center of soteriology; remember how Barth cannot bring himself to confess the full reality of the atonement, that Jesus Christ suffered in our place the punishment with which a holy God justly condemns us—not because he needed a sacrifice in order to be God, but because we needed our sins covered in order to be with him.

But here we must address ourselves to virtually an entire generation of theologians and biblical scholars, almost without exception. Where were the Old Testament scholars when talk was so loud about partnership with God? When talk was so loud about God empowering us to liberation? Where were the New Testament scholars when talk was so loud about building the kingdom? When talk was so loud about self-ful-fillment and self-worth? Indeed, where were the church his-torians, who had read Luther and Calvin? Who could not see that the church has faced this ideology before? Who could not at least tell us, in all historical honesty and objectivity, that the church once stood against this ideology, recogniz-ing that the gospel itself is at stake?

Instead, we hear, in an echo of the later Barth, about God's "story of salvation." And certainly I do not deny the histor-ical concreteness of the witness of Israel and the early church. But the story of salvation, we have been told, is God's common history with humanity, God's determined effort, again and again, to render humanity in right relationship to himself and to one another. Determined effort? Have they not heard? Do they not know that in Jesus Christ he has already done it? Have they utterly forgotten that Jesus Christ is God's one redemptive purpose in all creation? Have they no idea that Jesus Christ alone is the one salvation of God in both Testaments of Scripture?

And from the narrative theologians, we hear that we must merge our narrative with the narrative of Jesus in Scripture. Is this what they mean by faith in Jesus Christ? Do they not know that Jesus Christ is risen, and speaks for himself in his Word by his Spirit (Rom. 10; 1 Cor. 2)? And that he calls us to repentance and faith in him, putting us right with God freely by his mercy, rendering us a new creation by his Spirit, putting to death in us the sinful flesh through his blood (Rom. 8)? Is this a "merging of narratives"? When Paul says, "I have been crucified with Christ; it is no longer I who live, but Christ who lives in me" (Gal. 2:20), is this "finding our identity in the story of faith"?

Not only are the truths of the gospel not boldly professed, but they are often openly ridiculed, not only from the obvi-ous ideological left, but also from so-called Reformed bib-lical scholars and theologians. We are told that the call to personal repentance and faith in Jesus Christ is "fundamentalism." Was Calvin a fundamentalist? Was Luther a fundamentalist? We are told that the sovereign grace of God in salvation is to be rejected as hierarchical; and that, apparently for the sake of the feminist lobby, they must no longer speak of the kingdom of God, but only of the reign of God. But who does not see that if they are to change the language in the interests of women, it exposes the fact that their concept is grounded in their own self-interest? As if they have the right—they who are in "covenant-partnership" with God, who "share God's story"—to be so terribly concerned with excluding anyone? As if they could include anyone! Such a kingdom is not the kingdom of God.

The New Covenant

The church must recover in its teaching and preaching of the Word of God, what it discerns by faith in the Lord's Supper: the overwhelming good news, that God alone has done what we could not do, sending forth his Son as a sacrifice for sins, canceling the debt of sin, reconciling us to himself. We must proclaim the mystery of God's generosity and kindness, bearing witness to the free gift of his grace. We must also proclaim the necessary response of faith in order to receive the free gift, the faith that is itself the free gift of the Spirit, the faith that knows that we are surrounded, from beginning to end, by the bounty of Christ. He is the bread of life.

3

The Church

One, Holy, Catholic, and Apostolic

The liberation theologians and preachers seldom speak of "the church" except to say on occasion that "the church must die" for the sake of the coming reign of God. We are told that the reign of God is about the tearing down of walls of sexism, of racism, of classism, and the building of "community." Wherever community is being built, there is the reign of God.

This, I submit, is false doctrine. The church is not an instance of "community." According to Holy Scripture, "There is one body and one Spirit, just as you were called to the one hope that belongs to your call, one Lord, one faith, one baptism, one God and Father of us all, who is above all and through all and in all" (Eph. 4:4–6). The church of Jesus Christ participates in the scandal of particularity of its Lord.

Here again, the theological doublespeak among the liberation theologians is thick: we hear of "globalization," of "ecumenicity," and so forth; but what is meant is the worldwide
spread of "justice and peace"—the egalitarian ideological
agenda—even if the "institutional church" has to step aside,
which is just the opposite of belief in and work toward the
unity of the one church of Jesus Christ.

Just as fascism used the church to further its ideological
agenda, so the church is being used by egalitarianism to further its ideological agenda. But the liberation theologians,
like the German Christians before them, have made one fatal
miscalculation: Jesus of Nazareth is not dead but risen, and
speaks for himself in his Word by his Spirit. As Luther said
of the Devil, "one little word will fell him." The Spirit and his
gifts are ours, through him who with us sideth.

The Messianic Community

If it is not the church of Jesus Christ, what is the community that is fostered among liberation theologians and
preachers? Here again, we have only to listen closely to find
our answer.

An important clue is to be found in their understanding
and portrayal of the mission of the church. The traditional
mission of the church—the Great Commission to tell the
good news of Jesus Christ to the whole creation—is derided
and ridiculed as "fundamentalist" and "patriarchal" and
"exclusionary." This, we are told, is evangelism; what the liberation theologians and preachers tell us they are about is
"evangelization." What is evangelization? The building of
the reign of God on earth, the establishing of global justice
and peace.

But let us ask them further: What is this world of justice
and peace? It is a world in which the walls of hierarchy, of
sexism and racism and classism have been broken down.
But what is in its place, we ask? And here we run up against
the silent wall of liberation theologians and preachers. I've

got a dream! we are told. Tell us about that dream, we ask. And what we hear is simply an ideological nihilism, no different in kind from that of the fascists. The rhetoric is clearly different: then we had a thousand-year reign, now we have global community of peace and justice. But what is just as apparent is that the filling out of those terms is a function of the "empowerment" of those who wield the ideology. It is less obvious perhaps. Fascism openly excluded whole communities for the sake of its ideology. Egalitarianism is eager to welcome everyone, except those who maintain the evangelical faith in the one Lord, one faith, one baptism. Only these must go. But that is a community that excludes Jesus Christ, and therefore the community of Antichrist.

We are told by the liberation theologians and preachers that theirs is a messianic community. Where once Jesus preached the reign of God and lived by its rule in opposing all the hierarchies of his time, so today liberation theologians and preachers preach and live by the rule of the reign of God, seeking to extend its boundaries until it embraces all the world.

Now, what is the messianic community but a community of messiahs? Each liberation theologian and preacher is taking on the role of the Messiah, seeking to do in our day what Jesus did in his. But this is precisely the condition of which Jesus himself spoke: "Take heed that no one leads you astray. For many will come in my name, saying, 'I am the Christ,' and they will lead many astray" (Matt. 24:4–5). Here is a community in which each theologian and preacher is a self-attested messiah. Again, there are similarities and differences with fascism. The same language was used then—but it was of one figure only, Adolf Hitler. Now it is spread around among all the proponents of liberation theologians and preachers, and is covered over in theological doublespeak. But the diabolical claim is equally as unmistakable.

Where does it come from? Again, I suggest that the ideology is a direct outgrowth of the civil rights movement—

another "struggle" in the 1960s in North America. And here again one must point directly to the figure of Dr. Martin Luther King, Jr. His speeches attracted a nation, but who cannot now listen without the overwhelming sense of a self-attested messiah? That it was in the name of Jesus Christ, and in the environment of his church, makes no difference; the biblical text we have just quoted makes clear that the false messiahs will come in Jesus' name. But the sign of apostasy was King's failure to point to Jesus Christ as God's one act of salvation for the world, and his failure to maintain in his witness the scandal of particularity in which the church itself participates. King founded a cause, and a movement, which certainly arose in the environment of the believing community, but which quickly eliminated the witness of that community. That is, he maintained a cause of "community" that eliminated the truth. And that is the mark of a false prophet.

Was it not then King's followers who suggested, and still suggest, that the Letter from the Birmingham Jail be included in the canon of Scripture? Indeed, it is important that he had "followers," or "disciples"; the name itself is perhaps not objectionable, but the point certainly is: and that is that King became for his followers a rival to the one Lord, Jesus Christ. But that is to break, in a terrifying way, the first commandment: you shall have no other gods before me.

We hear from the liberation theologians and preachers that they are about "God's mission on earth," and that is the establishment of a world without hierarchy, as their version of a world of "peace and justice." But where is this in Holy Scripture? Where does Scripture ever tell us to break down the walls of hierarchy? The Law clearly commands us to care for the poor; it commands us not to oppress our neighbor or to rob him (Lev. 19:13) and enjoins upon us care for the widow, the orphan, the stranger who is within our gates. To do so is, indeed, "religion that is pure and undefiled before God" (James 1:27). It was on the basis of these texts and others, for example, that the Reformers spoke very consistently about the church's obligation to the poor. But liberation theology tells us that we must build a classless society, a world in which there are no poor people. That, we are told, is God's mission to the church. And the means to bring this about, we are told, is God's "preferential option for the poor." What is this but the affirmative-action ideology of the civil rights movement? Scripture itself says: "You shall do no injustice in judgment; you shall not be partial to the poor or defer to the great, but in righteousness shall you judge your neighbor" (Lev. 19:15). But if it is not in Scripture, where is it grounded? We are told by the liberation theologians and preachers, that just as God once spoke through the poor, so God is speaking through the poor today. But God never spoke through "the poor." God, the church has always recognized, spoke through the apostles and the prophets; many were indeed economically poor, but that is never appealed to as the basis for their witness. What is appealed to is simple: "thus says the Lord." Scripture alone contains true prophecy; all other claims are false prophecy.

The disciples of Jesus faced the issue of the messianism of a classless society, when Mary anointed the feet of Jesus with costly ointment of pure nard, wiping his feet with her hair. According to John's account, it was Judas Iscariot who responded: "Why wasn't this ointment sold, and the money given to the poor?" To which Jesus responded, that Mary was right and Judas was wrong; for she was anointing the true Messiah for his death and burial, while Judas was seeking to lead a mass-movement that would eliminate poverty. "The poor you always have with you, but you do not always have me." Mary knew him; Judas betrayed him (John 12:1–7, and parallels).

God's Mission in the World

How is it, we continue to inquire, that on virtually the same soil, the Barmen Declaration could confess against the encroachments of ideology into the faith of the church, while the 1967 Confession could wholeheartedly identify the gospel with an ideology? It is clear that what we now see as the heresies of the ecclesiology of liberation theology are simply more manifest forms of views of wide currency in the church, in particular among the Reformed churches in North America. What clearly stands behind the false doctrine of liberation theology is a fundamental role-reversal of Christ and the church. We are often told by the proponents of egalitarianism that "the church is to continue the ministry of Jesus." Just as Jesus came to "inaugurate" the reign of God, so we now are to continue his ministry in our ministry. Just as Jesus came to reconcile, so we, too, are now to reconcile. Just as Jesus came to redeem, so the community is now to be a redemptive community. And the Spirit has the role of "empowering" the community to this, its redemptive role.

Not even the late medieval church, for all its errors, went quite this far; perhaps a figure like Thomas Muentzer can stand as a historical example. For here is a monstrous confusion of the predicates of Christ with the predicates of the church, and an utter failure to carry out the ministry of the church. Because Jesus Christ has been combined with an ideology, the proponents of egalitarianism are neither hot nor cold; "For you say, I am rich, I have prospered, and I need nothing; not knowing that you are wretched, pitiable, poor, blind, and naked" (Rev. 3:17). In the name of Jesus, it professes itself to be the redeemer, which is sheer folly. There is only one answer: to repent and turn again, to remember that he does not hate or despise us, but loves us, and wants to be with us; that he calls us to repent and be zealous. "Behold, I stand at the door and knock; if any one hears my voice and opens the door, I will come in to him and eat with him, and he with me" (Rev. 3:20).

And here we must turn again to Karl Barth. For was it not Barth, shortly after the Second World War, who felt so sure that the word "church" needed to be replaced by the word "community"? Was it not Barth who came to speak of the church as the earthly-historical form of the existence of Jesus? Was it not Barth who continued to flirt with the concept of apokatastasis? The problem here is not the profound biblical witness that God sent his Son to die for the sins of the world; nor the profound biblical mystery of the Christian hope for the salvation of humankind. The problem is Barth's persistent downplaying of the necessary response of faith for receiving the free gift of salvation, and his characterization of the response as "acknowledgment." To be sure, Christians are to confess with their lips; but they are also to believe in their hearts and so be saved (Rom. 10:9). Christians are to be born again by the washing of regeneration and renewal in the Holy Spirit that God poured out upon us richly through Jesus Christ our Savior.

Moreover, it was Barth who so fused the Law and the gospel that he turned the gospel into Law and the Law into ideology. Already at Barmen it was the Lutheran theologians who insisted that Barmen 5 be added to counterbalance the appropriate biblical dialectic of Barmen 1. Indeed, Jesus Christ is the one Lord of the world. But the Law is not another form of the gospel. We often hear from Barth's school about the "claim of the gospel"; they are unaware that the gospel makes no claim, that it is sheer promise. But nor are they aware that those who belong to Jesus Christ, in whom the Holy Spirit dwells, are to be consecrated unto the service of God in the doing of his revealed will. It is the Christian, saved by grace through faith in the gospel, who knows that the Law—God's revealed will in his Word—is the Law of Christ, that it is Jesus' own command calling forth the response of obedience from those who are transformed by his mercy. Christians are not to conform to this world, whether cultural or countercultural, but be transformed by the renewal of their minds, that they may prove what is the will of God, what is good and acceptable and perfect.

It was Dietrich Bonhoeffer's *Cost of Discipleship* that exposed the cheap grace of cultural Christianity through its neglect of God's revealed will in his Word. Now we must likewise expose the ethical vacuousness of countercultural Christianity, through its identical neglect of God's revealed will in his Word.

Moreover, is it any surprise that a generation later, theologians in Barth's circle are deriding evangelism? Can only speak of "evangelization" that is the "building of a world of peace and justice"? They do not know the gospel—who among them speaks about acquittal at the judgment seat of God through the death of his Son?—but neither do they know the Law, imagining in their vanity that they have become a law unto themselves. And indeed they have.

Here again, a whole generation of theologians and biblical scholars, with very few exceptions, has ridiculed the faith of the church. Where Scripture makes clear the necessary response of faith, we are told by the proponents of egalitarian ideology that such a concern is "fundamentalism." It is ridiculed as "selfish concern for personal salvation." All the while, these so-called Christian leaders were speaking about themselves, about the church, as if they were the redeemer, the reconciler, the savior. Who, but they, cannot see their folly? A whole generation of "religious educators" who steered everything toward the "community inaugurated by Jesus" and away from Jesus Christ himself in his Word, and the life of discipleship by faith in him. A whole generation of pastoral care that invites people to healing by the "community" and knows nothing of the healing that comes through the shed blood of our Savior and Lord. Where were the church historians, especially of the Reformation? Had we not heard all this before? Were not the monastic communities terribly concerned with feeding the poor and the hungry? Were not they, too, so terribly proud to be apart from the "world," building the "community"? Had we not heard the inflated predicates of the church before? Who told us again about Luther? about Calvin? about the martyrs? And where were the biblical scholars? The egalitarian ideology tried to find support again and again in the Old Testament. Where were the Old Testament scholars, to point out that the Bible never associates care for the poor with the critique of orthodoxy, but always with its preservation and reestablishment? We have heard again and again from liberation theologians and preachers concerning the so-called prophetic principle contained in the Old Testament, God's supposed call to tear down all hierarchy. Where were the Old Testament scholars to point out that this is sheer ideology from the political left? That the standard of judgment in every prophet is never the "voice of the poor" or the "voice of the people" but God's revealed will in his Law? That God commands us, not to adopt an ideology, but literally to care for the poor, in obedience to his Word?

And where were the New Testament scholars? It is absolutely astonishing that we hear nothing from New Testament scholars about the necessary response of faith for salvation. Instead we hear, as the ideology would lead us to expect, that the often-used plural "you" means "the community." And now we hear that the early church was an "alternative community" founded over against the "evil structures of the world"; that the early "Jesus movement" was a "countercultural" movement in the ancient world. Who cannot see that this is the egalitarian ideology of the 1960s, complete with its persecution complexes, written onto the first century? Why do the New Testament scholars not tell us about Jesus Christ himself, about what he did for the salvation of the world? Why do the New Testament scholars not tell us about conversion, about being born again, about the work of the Holy Spirit in the heart of the believer? Why do they not tell us that he is risen, and speaks for himself in his Word?

And where were the "narrative theologians"? They, too, can tell us of nothing but forming "alternative communities," of being "resident aliens" in the world. They, too, can only talk about themselves, and not about what Christ has done for us, and the response of faith in him. They, too, have confused the predicates of Christ with the predicates of the church, thereby losing both the true understanding of the gospel and the true understanding of the church.

And where were the messianic spiritual directors, counseling others in their "spiritual journeys," calling others to "spirituality"? Are they telling us what Jesus Christ has done for us on the cross? Are they calling us to faith in him through the work of the Holy Spirit, obeying his will in his Word? "God does not care for much praying, but for right praying" (Luther). No, they, too, ridicule the faith of the church as "fundamentalism." And by their folly and pride they are withholding the true bread of life and the true cup of salvation.

And where were the theologians of retrieval? They certainly wanted to protect the interests of the church over against those who would destroy it; but who are they to protect the interests of the church? Could they not see that in seeking to protect the church, they were simply embracing another ideology? Or is it really another ideology? Who among the theologians of retrieval said no! to the egalitarian ideology? They were quick to respond with talk about the church when its existence seemed threatened; but did they not remember that its existence is never, absolutely never, threatened? Did they utterly forget the rock—the gospel—upon which Jesus, and he alone, will build his church (Matt. 16:18)?

Ministry of Word and Sacrament

The church must recover its zeal for the commission that the exalted Lord has given to the church: to proclaim what he, and he alone, has done for the reconciliation of the world on the cross. Through the power of the Holy Spirit alone, the church must preach the Word, calling for faith, and itself living by his rule.

4

Holy Scripture

Sola Scriptura

Like other heresies, liberation theology has taken a truth from the Christian faith and put it into an alien ideological context. The truth—that God embraces and invites the poor, the vulnerable, the afflicted, the downcast—is put into the false ideology of egalitarianism, thus yielding the twisting and distorting of the gospel that we are here considering. And again, like other heresies, there is an effort to show that the theology that results is based on the Bible. And so liberation theologians and preachers have accumulated a sizable exegetical literature, not unlike other heretical movements.

We have already seen, and will continue to show, that Scripture directly contradicts not just little points here and there, but the entire ideology of liberation theology. It is not to be found in Holy Scripture; indeed, the exact opposite of what is said is what the Christian church reads in its canon. Why is that?

The Christian church confesses that Scripture alone is the Word of God, that Scripture alone contains the rule of faith that alone governs the speech and action of the church and all its members. The Christian church confesses that each generation is called upon to respond afresh to the one gospel as it is attested for us in Holy Scripture; and that the role of the Holy Spirit is to undercut all personal, political, and cultural agendas, bringing us face to face with Jesus Christ himself addressing us in his Word, in sovereign freedom, calling for the obedience of faith.

In all these ways, liberation theology is a defection from the faith of the Christian church. It has combined the Bible with the alien egalitarian ideology of the Enlightenment; it has called the Spirit what is in fact the prevailing ideological climate of the age. It utterly refuses to find in Scripture, and Scripture alone, the one rule of faith in the church of Jesus Christ, thus showing itself as a counterfeit faith.

The Ideological Sense

Brevard Childs has shown us in his *Biblical Theology of the Old and New Testaments* what every Christian reader of Scripture experiences daily: that Scripture has been shaped to address future generations of the people of God with the living reality of God. The Christian church confesses that Scripture alone is the vehicle through which the Holy Spirit brings us by faith to encounter the risen Christ. The church approaches Scripture in fervent anticipation, in the context of prayer, worship, awe, and reverence, asking our heavenly Father to open our hearts and minds by his Spirit, that we might hear Jesus Christ himself in his Word. With overwhelming joy and gratitude, the church responds in the obedience of faith, amazed at the divine answer to our prayer, striving again to obey his command to seek him in his Word, trusting in his promise.

This encounter with the living Lord in his Word the Reformers called the literal sense, which is the verbal sense of Holy Scripture in living unity with its one subject matter, who is Jesus Christ. Childs has shown us that Scripture is shaped for this purpose. Moreover, it is the daily experience of the Christian church that Scripture does indeed function in this way, that Scripture is clear and certain when grasped in faith, sometimes setting parameters outside of which is not the gospel, sometimes calling for discernment in the ongoing response of faith. It was Calvin in particular who pointed out that where Scripture alone is not the norm, there will be confusion, there will be error, there will be apostasy. And there will also be the wretched plea: yes, the Scripture is authoritative—but it is our context that guides us in understanding its meaning! How can any text have meaning apart from the context in which it is read?

And that is exactly the plea we hear from the liberation theologians and preachers. Most are willing in some sense to ascribe authority to the Bible. And yet we are told that "contextualization" means that each of us, each "community of readers," must come to interpret the Bible in the light of his or her context. We are told that the theologian is to "construe" the Bible based on its "use" within the "community." We are also often told, as if it is self-evident, that the historical-critical method mandates this "hermeneutic."

What is called "contextualization" is simply the prevailing ideology of egalitarianism. The effect of this "hermeneutical circle" is to render the liberation theologian or preacher unaccountable to the direct authority of Holy Scripture in the church. Appeal to the historical-critical method among them is deceptive, for the historical-critical method has shown, to those of faith, that Scripture is shaped for the purpose of laying a direct claim of truth upon the Christian church, calling for the response of faith, which is to affirm the truth of the Word, living by its rule. The "hermeneutical circle" has rendered liberation theologians blind to the truth of the Word. "Contextualization" is simply more strange theological doubletalk, disguising the fact that they have become a law unto themselves, false prophets claiming to speak God's Word but telling lies.

Once again, it is very common to hear among liberation theologians and preachers scorn and ridicule for the faith of the church. It is "fundamentalism," we are told, to affirm the direct authority of Holy Scripture in the church. Much like other heresies, a favorite grab-bag of a few selected, and completely misrepresented, biblical texts will be offered as "biblical support" for their views. Who indeed is the fundamentalist? Who is more egregiously guilty of proof-texting than the liberation theologians and preachers? When confronted with the overwhelming and clear testimony of Scripture pointing in the opposite direction, who is more utterly unable and unwilling to sustain a theological discussion on texts of Holy Scripture? Liberation theologians and preachers simply withdraw into the subterfuge of "contextualization," which is simply a shield from the living reality of God, a blind evasion of the truth.

The Hermeneutics of Evasion

Once again, one must notice in dismay that behind the obvious, surface abuse of Scripture lies a virtual generation of biblical scholarship and theology. It is not surprising—though it is utterly dismaying—that liberation theologians and preachers could so openly mishandle the text of Holy Scripture, with almost no serious response from the biblical and theological community, for the sad fact is that the egalitarian ideology that has attempted to smother the gospel has come precisely from the biblical and theological community.

Did we not hear from the theological community, and indeed from circles supposedly of a Reformed theological understanding, that the theologian must "construe" the

Bible based on its "use" within the community of faith? But here the Christian church sees the same problem that Calvin saw so clearly: What if it is being abused ideologically in the "community of faith"? Is not the theologian's "construal" then simply an ideological self-justification of the mishearing of the text? And indeed, that is exactly the impact this view has had, giving a whole generation license to pervert and twist Scripture at will, always appealing in the final analysis to the "community." But the Christian church, when it faces heresy, does not appeal in the final analysis to "the community," but to Jesus Christ as he is attested for us in Holy Scripture alone. It does so, because it lives by one faith and one faith only: Jesus is not dead, but risen, and speaks for himself in his Word by his Spirit.

Here again, we must return to the figure of Barth. For all his attempt to take the Bible seriously, the impression that his biblical exegesis leaves on the reader (with some notable exceptions) is of a virtuosic performance, unrepeatable as if by intention. How completely different from the exegesis of the Reformers! And how incommensurate with Scripture itself, which is shaped precisely to address each new generation with the living reality of the one gospel. Was it not Barth's exegesis that left a generation with the impression that the Scripture has no perspicuity, that it must be run through the mill of "imaginative construal" before it speaks? Indeed, it is clear especially in the later volumes of the *Church Dogmatics* that "imaginative construal" became a kind of natural theology in Barth, a literary-aesthetic natural theology. *Bundesgeschichte* was not only a theological category that twisted the subject matter of Scripture; it also functioned as a license for a generation of theologians and biblical scholars searching for "images" and "themes" and "symbols." And so one could finally rest one's case on reading the Bible as a "realistic novel." Who can now wonder, if this is the way the Bible was being read, how it could come about that virtually no one could say no to liberation theology, and in most cases simply joined the chorus? Or indeed, led the way!

And where were the biblical scholars? The problem does not lie in the historical-critical method, for it has shown, as Childs has made clear, for those who know how to use it in the church of Jesus Christ, the stance of the biblical literature itself as the Scripture of the church. The problem lies, rather, in the simple fact that the historical-critical method has been placed into the service of the egalitarian ideology of the Enlightenment. The historical study of the Bible has shown us, historically, that the Bible was shaped to exercise just the authority that the church of Jesus Christ knows, by faith in him, that it does in fact exercise. And yet the historical-critical "community" is the first to defend the false doctrine that it is the "community" that gives life to the text of the Bible. Can we not now see their self-deluding blindness? The irony is that the biblical scholar could be standing face to face with a text of Holy Scripture that the Christian reader knows is a direct denial of the ideology being espoused, and simply misunderstand and misrepresent it entirely. How otherwise can it be that Old Testament scholars did not say no to the vain distortion of Exodus misleading a virtual generation? How many listened when they were reminded of the golden calf that was created by "liberated" and "empowered" Israel? How many heard when they told again of the Law of God to which Israel was bound in covenant? Who among the New Testament scholars even whispered that there is not a word about "building the kingdom of God"?

And where were those who sought to focus on the "interpretation" of the Bible in serious engagement with the life of the church? They, too, were lost in the search for "patterns" and "themes" and "structures" and "symbols," organized loosely around a "story of faith." Did they not see that it is their "community" that "tells the story"? Had they utterly forgotten the overwhelming and joyful conviction of both Testaments of Scripture, and the church who lives by them, that we have a God who speaks to us in his Word? As they searched blindly for the "unity" of the Bible in its "diversity," had they forgotten completely that he is not dead, but risen? That Jesus Christ himself is the one subject matter of Holy Scripture, Old and New Testaments? Where was the "interpretation" of the Old Testament, in light of the clear confession of Scripture (Luke 24:27) that the risen Lord shows us a witness of himself in the Law and the Prophets and the Psalms? As they scorned and ridiculed the attempts of others to make good on this command and promise, did they completely forget that "the LORD has them in derision" (Ps. 2:4)?

And what about the "cultural-linguistic" approach to doctrine? Why did they not say no when it was time to say no? Neither could they appeal, as the church of Jesus Christ appeals, to the clear teaching of Holy Scripture as the resounding no! to false doctrine within the church. Again, how utterly different from the Reformers. Had they forgotten completely Luther's response to Erasmus, that Scripture makes assertions? Where were their assertions? Did they remove from their memory entirely Luther's statement that the Holy Spirit is not a skeptic? Why didn't they speak boldly? Why did they often sound like skeptics? Had they misunderstood entirely the Reformation recognition that the authority of the church is grounded in the authority of the Word, and never, absolutely never, the reverse? Was their "cultural-linguistic community" really so different from the "world"? Is it not now clear that it shares the very egalitarian ideology of the openly "liberated" theologians, which seeks a community ultimately grounded in itself, unaccountable to the authority of the Word?

The Canonical Authority of Scripture

The church must recover its reliance upon the canonical authority of Holy Scripture alone. It must recover basic assumptions concerning the reading of Scripture as canon, assumptions that have been neglected or forgotten. The church must pray for illumination by the Holy Spirit, who alone makes teachers and preachers of the Word. The church must pray that God will send out workers into the harvest, for the harvest is plentiful and the workers are few.

5

The Identity of God

The Hallowing of God's Name

Liberation theologians and preachers betray their fundamental apostasy from the Christian faith by their profanation of God's holy name: Father, Son, and Holy Spirit. We are told by the egalitarian ideology that God cannot be addressed as Father, that Jesus cannot be called the Son of God, for that would be "patriarchal." And, of course, behind the objections is the fundamental view of liberation theology: that human beings name God.

According to the witness of Scripture, this is blasphemy. God alone names himself in sovereign freedom and grace, condescending to share the most precious gift of his name with those whom he has called to be his own (Exod. 3:13–15). Jesus is given the name that is above every name; and he declares to us the name of the First Person of the Trinity, and in so doing discloses his own filial relation to the Father. He commands us to address him as our Father, and to pray for the hallowing of his name. In his own priestly prayer for the church, the church's one priest, Jesus Christ our Lord, identifies the unity of the church with the name that he has revealed: "Holy Father, keep them in thy name, which thou hast given me, that they may be one, even as we are one" (John 17:11). And it is the Holy Spirit himself who brings to the lips of the children of God: Abba! Father! (Rom. 8:15). Liberation theologians and preachers are preaching and teaching false doctrine; they are profaning the name of our God. Those who do not address God as Father are schismatic; they have broken away from the church, rejecting the name that was given to them by grace alone at baptism (Matt. 28:19). Those who do not profess Jesus Christ as the incarnate Son of God have neither the Son nor the Father (1 John 2:22–23). They speak, not from the Holy Spirit, the Spirit of truth, but from the spirit of error, which is the spirit of Antichrist (1 John 4:1–6).

The Idolatry of Ideology

We are told by the preachers and teachers of liberation theology that we must use "inclusive language" of God. No one human "naming" of God is to be given preference over any other "naming." The reason given is that all "namings" are symbols of human experience, and since the ideology of egalitarianism seeks to uplift the validity of human experience, the wealth of human symbols of God must be celebrated.

According to Holy Scripture, this is to replace the confession of the one true God with the "celebration" of idolatry. God is not known through the "symbolization" of human experience—the equivalent in the strange theological doublespeak of liberation theology to what Scripture calls an idol—but through the revelation of his name. The early church recognized the threat to the knowledge of God's reality revealed in Holy Scripture when it confessed the doctrine of the Trinity, one God in three persons, over against the many heresies in the ancient church. In particular, it confessed the one true God over against the gnostics of antiquity, who, like the liberation theologians and preachers, twisted and distorted the name of God through idolatrous worship of "symbols" of their own experience.

Here, of course, liberation theologians and preachers are continuing the long tradition of Protestant liberalism, with its fatal quest for human self-transcendence in the "symbols" of religion. Furthermore, it is no accident that liberation theology is so often linked with the ideology of process theology, which has its roots in the same soil. According to Isaiah 40, idolatry and process theology go hand in hand. It is the idolater, the one who makes his own gods from his own experience, who has utterly forgotten that God is the Creator of heaven and earth, the everlasting God, who does not faint or grow weary. It is the one who addresses God as Father in the obedience of faith in Jesus Christ, who knows that our Father knows what we need before we ask him (Matt. 6:8).

Nor is it any surprise to hear from the liberation theologians and preachers that behind the various symbols of God is the unknown. Much like the older liberalism, the current form is ultimately a form of nihilism, refusing with the left hand as well as with the right to raise hands of praise to the one true God in utter gratitude, awe, wonder, and joy, receiving in humility and reverence the overwhelming gift of his most holy name.

Finally, it is clear in Scripture that care for the poor is grounded in the recognition of God's reality disclosed in his name. "He who oppresses a poor man insults his Maker, but he who is kind to the needy honors him" (Prov. 14:31). God does not command us to build a classless society; God does not, therefore, command us to discharge our obligation to the poor through ideological talk. Jesus' command, in keeping with the Law, is clear and unmistakable: "Give to him who begs from you, and do not refuse him who would borrow from you" (Matt. 5:42). Only those who know Jesus Christ recognize the claim to concrete deeds of love and mercy. Those who talk about a classless society mock the poor and insult their Maker (Prov. 17:5).

Taking God's Name in Vain

Liberation theologians and preachers are guilty of blasphemy and profanation of God's holy name. But behind the obvious abuse of God's name is a subtler form of abuse, which is itself a violation of God's commandment not to take his name in vain. It is easier to detect outright blasphemy, though its frequency and flagrancy among liberation theologians and preachers can desensitize one to its reality, somewhat like the frequency of violence on television. But the misuse of God's name that has surfaced so dramatically in the teaching and preaching of liberation theology goes back several years, and involves a virtual generation of theologians and biblical scholars.

Here again we must turn to the theology of Karl Barth. For it was Barth who, in the later volumes of the *Church Dogmatics*, sought to house the person and work of Jesus Christ in the larger framework of a history of the covenant. But that is to reverse the basic witness of Scripture, which is that it is from the person and work of Jesus Christ himself that we learn the meaning and truth of salvation. God's saving righteousness, professes Paul, is revealed in the gospel: "For I am not ashamed of the gospel: it is the power of God for salvation to every one who has faith, to the Jew first and also to the Greek. For in it the righteousness of God is revealed from faith to faith; as it is written, 'He who through faith is righteous shall live'" (Rom. 1:16–17). Perhaps the best modern formulation of this issue is the point: revelation is not a predicate of history, but history is a predicate of revelation. It is sad to remember that it was Karl Barth himself who so brilliantly made this point in the years of his opposition to the German Christians.

But the consequences of this reversal, in Barth and so many others of the past thirty years, are devastating. It has unleashed a virtual flood of false doctrine among theologians and biblical scholars, leaving the door wide open for the ideology of egalitarianism to erode and consume the confession of faith during this era, with very few exceptions. The natural theology of partnership—Barth's *Bundesgeschichte*—has twisted and distorted the confession of faith, in the end defecting completely from the gospel.

We have already seen that it brings with it a denial of Jesus Christ, through a denial of the scandal of particularity. But now we must also observe the obscene effects it has on the confession of the identity of God. Along with the blasphemy of God's name has come a more subtle dishonoring of his holy name, less noticeable, but all the more insidious. A virtual generation has operated with a gnostic natural theology of the Trinity. God, we are so often told, is a "partnership," and God seeks to establish partnership between "Godself" and humanity, and seeks to establish partnership among human beings, and in the whole cosmos. Jesus, we are told, announced this divine cause, and was willing to give his life, vanquished by the hierarchical forces of evil, in its service. Now, many continue to worship God with their lips—they want to use the doctrine of the Trinity—but would like to change the names to Creator, Redeemer, Sustainer, or the like, or to address Jesus as the "Wisdom of God." Along with the errors of modalism and subordinationism, they betray the fact that for them, the Trinity is a symbol of the ideology of "partnership," necessary perhaps as a justification for their cause, but amenable to necessary changes when the cause itself requires it. This is to take the name of the Lord in vain. The case is similar among those who exult in the divine "process," in the triune "being in its becoming," only to talk of God's "open future," thus denying the

Alpha and the Omega, Jesus Christ. Here, the Trinity has
become a symbol for the ideology of historical "process,"
which is surely the same cause with a different name. This,
too, is to take the Lord's name in vain. It is to worship him
with the lips, but not with the heart. And the commandment
makes clear: the Lord will not hold him guiltless who takes
his name in vain.

The dishonoring comes through the failure to approach
the reality of God through faithful response to his self-rev-
elation in Jesus Christ. It is only by faith in Jesus Christ, by
encountering Christ in his Word heard in faith through the
power of the Spirit, that the church knows the reality of God
as Father, Son, and Spirit. Other avenues to the triune God,
even in an effort to maintain its truth, are sooner or later
exposed for what they are: the false teaching of ideology that
contradicts and despises the faith of the church.

The fatal reversal of the history of salvation and the person of Jesus Christ that we have observed in Barth was, of
course, widely shared by others. It was the basic mistake in
the theology of Reinhold Niebuhr who, though he bravely
stood up against communism, in his own espousal of the
cause of socialism and his denial of the scandal of particularity showed that for him, too, Christianity had devolved
into an ideology. The irony is that Barth ended up sounding
much like Albrecht Ritschl—is there really much difference
in the spread of "co-humanity" and *Reichgottesarbeit?*—
while Niebuhr ended up sounding much like Walter
Rauschenbusch. And the story is little different with figures
like Jürgen Moltmann, who in the end makes the same reversal and espouses the same egalitarian cause.

But where were the biblical scholars while this was going
on? Where were the Old Testament scholars to tell us that
this was precisely the sin of Israel and the golden calf, seeking to "name" God from their "experience of liberation"
rather than adhering in the obedience of faith to the God
who bound them in covenant to his revealed will? Where

were the heralds of the "Interpretation" of the Bible, seeking as they were to read off of the Old Testament the so-called kingdom of God, thus utterly bypassing the basic Christian confession of faith: Jesus-Kyrios? How can it be that it is precisely among Old Testament scholars that we now hear that "God is a suffering God," that God's reality is inside, rather than outside, his amazing love for the world? Did they utterly forget everything?

Where were the New Testament scholars? Why did they not tell us that "partnership" is not the center of history, but the cross of Jesus Christ? That God sent his only-begotten Son, not as the martyr to a good cause—"get thee behind me Satan"—but as an atoning sacrifice for the sins of the world? That God acted for us, not because he needed a sacrifice in order to be God, but because we needed our sins to be covered? That God loves us freely, of his good pleasure, not because he is not God without us?

The ideology of egalitarianism has blinded the biblical scholarship of virtually a generation. But we must further point out that even in ecclesial circles where there is some effort to retain allegiance to the name of God, it is grounded, not in the reality of faith in Jesus Christ as he addresses us in his Word, but in the nature of the ecclesial community. In some fashion or another, appeal is made to the worshiping community for the basic warrant of adherence to God's name. But the true worshiping community, in Scripture, and in the church of Jesus Christ that gathers around the Word, is always a response to the self-declaration of God's revealed name in his Word. There is a subtle, but catastrophic difference, between worshiping the doctrine of the Trinity and worshiping the triune God. The theologian, too, is asked: Do you love me more than these?

The Name of God

In deepest humility, the church must remember that God's name is highly exalted above all things, that God's name is enthroned upon the praises of his people. The one eternal God—Father, Son, and Spirit—is not mocked. Those who address him by his name must seek to hallow it; and those who address the one holy God, are themselves called to be his holy people. The Christian is given God's name at baptism to signify that I am no longer my own, but the Lord's, for I have been bought with a price. In all that I do, I must honor and glorify God's name, doing everything in the name of the Lord Jesus, giving thanks to God the Father through him, praying in the Spirit at all times.

6

Faith

By Faith Alone

Late medieval doctrine, for all its semi-Pelagianism, at least made a pretense of justification by grace through faith. There was at least talk of "faith formed by love" and so forth. But liberation theologians and preachers have dropped all pretense. They simply do not talk about faith at all. Faith has been entirely replaced by "the praxis of love." As Scripture makes abundantly clear, this is the denial of the gospel through works-righteousness, for we are saved, not by works of the Law (summarized in the twofold love command), but by grace alone through faith alone apart from all works of the Law. It is as if liberation theologians and preachers are utterly unaware that Paul exists in the canon; and they therefore twist and distort every other part of the canon as well.

Liberation theologians have removed the stumbling block of the cross. They seek a salvation by works of the Law. They spurn the blood of Jesus Christ our Savior, who alone puts us right with God through his sacrifice on the cross. They despise the free gift of his grace, to be received by faith alone. Nor do they teach the mortification of the flesh through the efficacy of Christ's blood. They do not know, what the Christian knows, that the old self has been crucified with Christ, so that the sinful flesh might be destroyed. Neither do they know that we, who were dead in sin, God made alive together with Christ, freed by the Spirit to obey the Law of Christ. Because they seek salvation by works of the Law, they do not understand the Law of which they speak. The Law has worked sin and death in them apart from faith in Christ; and so the perverse shadow of the Law, the ideology of "partnership," has become sheer lawlessness (2 Thess. 2:1–12).

Ideology as Natural Theology

The theology of the Christian church is based on the Word of God heard in faith. The egalitarian ideology of liberation theology is based on what it calls "human experience." As Romans 1 professes, the distinction is clear and devastating in its consequences. It is in the gospel that God's saving righteousness is revealed, from faith to faith (Rom. 1:17), the gospel that is the preaching of Christ heard in faith (Rom. 10), in words that the Spirit teaches and that are discerned by the work of the Spirit (1 Cor. 2).

Liberation theology, like every other ideology, is based on the resources of human experience, which is to say the resources of the flesh, which is to say the resources of human sin. In particular, is the counterfeit gospel of the civil rights movement, the false gospel of human self-fulfillment. "I am somebody!" is the basic confession of the liberation gospel. And, indeed, this is the basic confession of the "community" of liberation theologians and preachers. Where the false apostles declare, "I am somebody!" the true apostle declared,

"Christ died for our sins" (1 Cor. 15:3 and context). The latter preaches Christ, the former preaches Antichrist. The essence of this particular natural theology, as of all natural theology, is the failure to honor God as God and to give thanks to him. The cry of egalitarian ideology is the cry of utter revolt against the Creator, known by faith in Jesus Christ alone. It is a rejection of God and a rejection of God's Messiah. It is therefore accompanied by its own messiahs, most notably the person of Dr. Martin Luther King, Jr. How utterly, inconceivably different, was the witness of the black church during and after the Civil War, and the pseudoliturgy of the civil rights movement. From the former came hymns of praise, thanksgiving, and wonder at the amazing grace of God; from the latter came a liturgy of worship to self-proclaimed christs, accompanied by ideological anger and blame. What was missing entirely—the essence of all natural theology—was the honoring of God and giving thanks to him. The movement exchanged the truth about God for a lie. It worshiped and served the creature—"I am somebody!"—rather than the Creator, who is blessed forever. The only real difference from most previous forms of natural theology is that here it is open and undisguised. Here, natural theology has become systematic theology. It no longer hides in the shadow of the prophets and apostles—though it has hacked with axes the wooden trellis of God's holy church—but now openly proclaims its own pseudo-messianic intentions. It has its own counterfeit-apostolic kerygma, its own "community," its own "ministers," its own "mission in the world" that it heralds as "God's mission," its own quest for "globalization." It is the sheer lie of the Antichrist.

"Therefore God gave them up in the lusts of their hearts to impurity, to the dishonoring of their bodies among themselves" (Rom. 1:24). It is no surprise that the rise of the egalitarian ideology of the civil rights movement was accompanied by the so-called sexual revolution. Notice the point of

Paul's witness: he does not say that God will judge because of sexual misconduct, but rather that sexual misconduct, the using and abusing of one another for self-gratification, is the sign of God's judgment. Claiming to be wise, they have become fools, and so God has given them up to their "partnership."

Ideology as Confession

Here we must return again to the extraordinary fact that the egalitarian ideology of the civil rights movement was confessionally enshrined in the literature of the Presbyterian Church. And here again we must notice with dismay the influence of Karl Barth. For it was in the later work of Barth in particular that he fatally reversed the relation between the history of salvation and the person and work of Jesus Christ, thus unleashing a drive toward false doctrine in the churches under his influence. What Barth called the "history of the covenant" became a literary-ethical "symbol," to which he sought to attach the living reality of Jesus Christ. But, as he himself once taught, this is to violate the first commandment.

Again, why did faith virtually drop out of the vocabulary of liberation theology? Here again, we must return to Barth. For in the later volumes of the *Dogmatics,* faith is described as "acknowledgment" of the gospel. It is no wonder that Paul was no longer read among the liberation theologians, for how short of the Pauline witness does this fall! It is no wonder that in the place of Christian confessional theology will come a virtual generation of gnostic natural theology, if this is how faith is understood.

And indeed, already in Barth salvation is described as the "definitive fulfillment of the creature by God"; already in Barth the essence of being human is described as "co-humanity"; already in Barth sin is described as an "episode" in the "covenant-partnership" of humanity with God; already in Barth is his astonishing periodic endorsement of

Tillich's symbolic view of a "God above God," the nihilistic shadow of gnostic natural theology, seeking as it does to evade the living reality of God in his Word.

In the wake of Barth's theology came a virtual generation of gnostic natural theology in the church, centered around the ideology of "partnership." In particular, is the perversion of the cross of Jesus Christ. We are told concerning the "symbol" of the cross that Jesus was willing to give his life for the cause of partnership. But this is false doctrine of a counterfeit faith. Jesus Christ, Scripture professes, died for our sins. It is we, indeed I (Rom. 7), the whole of humanity, who have fallen short of the glory of God. God so loved the world that he gave his only-begotten Son as a sacrifice for our sins. Jesus did not die a martyr's death to a cause; but, in fulfillment of the divine plan of salvation for the world, he was crucified, offered up by the hands of sinful Israel, an atoning sacrifice for the sins of the world. Those who portray otherwise "crucify the Son of God on their own account and hold him up to contempt" (Heb. 6:6).

And here we must remark on the view of sin in liberation theology and preaching. Much like the older liberalism and the social gospel, liberation theology locates sin in the "evil structures of society," in particular in the form of "hierarchy." Like the older social gospel, liberation theologians dismiss the view of Scripture—that all have sinned and fallen short of the glory of God, that sin is my personal predicament as a rebel, an affront to God, turning my back to God and not my face—as "fundamentalism." They have utterly forgotten that sin brings with it objective guilt before God, and know nothing of the forgiveness of sin in Jesus Christ, who "canceled the bond which stood against us with its legal demands; this he set aside, nailing it to the cross." They have stumbled over the stumbling block of the cross in their unbelief, and so are utterly blind to the good news of God's amazing grace. But in liberation theology, the ideology has emerged in full bloom. Salvation is a matter of recovering "psychic wholeness"; it is a releasing of the potential of the human self that has been trapped in the "evil world" of hierarchy. The biblical view, that the structure of society is God's check on the evil of human sin (Rom. 13:1–7), is twisted and turned around—the entrapped self is innocent, and the evil structures are to be abolished to liberate the inner self. It is this suffering inner self that is the new basis for the knowledge of God, the new gnostic natural theology. Above all, the fall is to be directly denied. Here there is no pretense; liberation theologians, indeed, a virtual generation of theologians and biblical scholars, have either dismissed the fall or read it as a gnostic "symbol" of human self-alienation. And of course they must, for it is the witness to the fall, known by faith in Jesus Christ (Rom. 5), which directly denies the basis for their theology that human beings have access to the reality of God through their experience. For we are by nature children of wrath, and the natural theology that results incurs God's wrath. Moreover, the fall tells us, what they cannot hear, that we are both utterly accountable for our sin and utterly unable to remedy it.

Similarly is the cross as a "symbol" for the Christian life. We are told by the adherents of the egalitarian ideology that "bearing the cross" means changing from an egoistic self to an altruistic self, living in "solidarity" with one's neighbor, fulfilling the claim of partnership. But change based on what? Our ability to change! And what is our ability to change but the gospel of self-fulfillment that lies at the heart of the ideology of egalitarianism. They have utterly forgotten the witness of Scripture, that we are dead in our sins; that the cross is not a symbol for self-improvement through partnership, but the efficacious blood of Jesus Christ himself who, through the work of the Spirit, puts to death in us the old man, creating us anew in his image, thus doing what we cannot do. They have utterly forgotten their baptism.

God, we are told, "empowers" us to partnership. But apart from faith in Jesus Christ, apart from baptism into his death and new life in him, what is being "empowered" is simply the flesh, the sinful self. The result then is not the fruit of the Spirit, which is love, but the works of the flesh, covered by the ideology of partnership. Here is an ideology that is still stuck in the predicament attested in Romans 7, trying to be saved by the Law. "Grace" means God's empowerment of the self—*infusio gratiae!*—and God's benevolent willingness to overlook the stringency of the Law, to "forgive" our failures—*facientibus quod in se est, Deus non negat gratiam!* But they have utterly forgotten that those who live under the Law are bound to keep the whole Law. "You are severed from Christ, you who would be justified by the law; you have fallen away from grace" (Gal. 5:4). They know neither the justification (there is therefore now no condemnation for those who are in Christ Jesus) nor the sanctification (for the law of the Spirit of life in Christ Jesus has set me free for the law of sin and death) which comes by faith in Jesus Christ our Lord.

The "symbol" of the cross, we are told, symbolizes martyrdom to the cause of "partnership" throughout the world. How utterly different from the martyrdom of disciples of Jesus Christ. The ideology of partnership displays the morbid fanaticism that lies at the root of every ideology. It is an ideology feeding upon the "anger" of its adherents—which Paul includes as a manifest work of the flesh (Gal. 5:20). But to his own disciples, Jesus says: "Behold, I have given you authority to tread upon serpents and scorpions, and over all the power of the enemy; and nothing shall hurt you. Nevertheless do not rejoice in this, that the spirits are subject to you; but rejoice that your names are written in heaven" (Luke 10:19–20). The joy of the Lord is despised by the adherents of the egalitarian ideology; they ridicule it as "fundamentalism" and despise it as "selfishness," thereby betraying the fact that they simply have no idea.

Because they know nothing of biblical faith, liberation theologians and preachers openly despise and ridicule biblical hope. Here again, hope is the "symbol" for human self-fulfillment; and God is called upon as the "empowering" of our agency toward fulfillment. Did they utterly forget everything? They have no idea of the hope of the Christian, grounded in God's saving act in the cross and resurrection of Jesus Christ, and his promised return, and grasped through the Word heard in faith, sealed on our hearts by the Spirit as a down payment. For them, if there is a resurrection at all, it is the many "resurrections" symbolically present in the "globalization" of the ideology of egalitarianism. They are most to be pitied, for they really have no idea of the true hope of the Christian. Because they dismiss Christ crucified, neither do they know Christ risen from the grave, the world's only hope.

The egalitarian ideology of many in the mainline churches is false doctrine, resting on the basis of natural theology. According to Paul in Romans 1, there are further consequences: "For this reason God gave them up to dishonorable passions. Their women exchanged natural relations for unnatural, and the men likewise gave up natural relations with women and were consumed with passion for one another, men committing shameless acts with men and receiving in their own persons the due penalty for their error" (vv. 26–27). Notice again this point: Paul does not say that homosexuality is the cause or the occasion of God's judgment, but the sign of God's judgment. It is in this light that we now recall the fact that it was in the Presbyterian Church that a serious overture was recently made for the ordination of homosexuals. The very sign of God's judgment, the ultimate twisting and distorting of our creatureliness, the veritable pseudosacrament of natural theology, was seriously introduced for consideration in the good order of Christ's church. Is this not the desolating sacrilege (Matt. 24:15)? Do we not see here the ultimate depravity of the "kerygma" of liberation theology? Is this not the crowning glory of "I am somebody"? There really is a very short line indeed from the Confession of 1967 to the overture for the ordination of homosexuals in the Presbyterian Church. What started out as ideology has ended up as self-deluding blasphemy.

The Stumbling Block of the Cross

From its inception the church of Jesus Christ has been tempted to remove the stumbling block of the cross, to reject the Messiah for messianism. The church is tempted to replace the gospel with an ideology for the masses. But in the end, it was the masses who cried, "Crucify him!" In the end, it was the "people" who called for the release of Barabbas the liberator. And in the end, it was a little maid—so great is the hold of an ideology—who was the occasion for Peter to deny Christ three times. Jesus' words to Peter, and the disciples, and the multitudes, are his words to us now: "If any man would come after me, let him deny himself and take up his cross and follow me. . . . For whoever is ashamed of me and my words in this adulterous and sinful generation, of him will the Son of man also be ashamed, when he comes in the glory of his Father with the holy angels" (Mark 8:35, 38). The church's response to the loss of faith in our generation is not fresh encouragement to "have more faith." It is, in the obedience of faith, to preach Christ crucified for the sins of the world, a stumbling block to unbelief, but to faith the power of God unto salvation.

7

False Doctrine

Church Discipline

According to Scripture, God lays claim to his people: "You shall be holy, for I am holy" (Lev. 11:44–45; 1 Pet. 1:16). This fundamental claim has been recognized in the doctrine of the Christian church as the mark of holiness. The Reformers, when asked what marks the church as the church, usually responded: the right preaching of the gospel and the right celebration of the sacraments. However, what is often forgotten is that the Reformers—Calvin in particular—also included church discipline as a true mark of the church.

Heresy is not only a twisting and distorting of the content of the gospel; it is also known by its fruits. According to Jesus, "Beware of false prophets, who come to you in sheep's clothing but inwardly are ravenous wolves. You will know them by their fruits. Are grapes gathered from thorns, or figs from thistles? So, every sound tree bears good fruit, but the bad tree bears evil fruit. A sound tree cannot bear evil fruit, nor can a bad tree bear good fruit. Every tree that does not bear good fruit is cut down and thrown into the fire. Thus you will know them by their fruits" (Matt. 7:15–20). I have presented the claim that liberation theology is false prophecy, that it is preaching another gospel. I shall now consider what light is shed upon the works of the liberation preachers and teachers by this Word of Christ.

Theological Fascism

According to the Barmen Declaration, one of the marks of the German Christian heretics was the use of "force and insincere practices." In particular, it was through a variety of "teaching methods and actions" of the German Christians, seeking to enforce their views upon the church, that their heretical nature was exposed to view. The same can now be said of the "liberation" Christians, who seek to impose upon the church the egalitarian ideology that they espouse, who despise and ridicule the faith of the church, but, like wolves in the midst of sheep, prey upon it.

We are all aware of their efforts. In previous movements within the church, when fresh life was breathed into the church, its liturgy was enriched by new hymns and liturgical forms. But the liberation theologians and preachers betray their deception, for they will not rest content to offer new hymns for the church's consideration; they seek rather to substantially suppress the liturgy of the church through the use of so-called inclusive language. We hear that hymns must eliminate "gratuitous references to Lord," for they have rejected the One who bought us with the price of his own blood. We hear that we must no longer sing to our Father, for they have turned their backs to him and not their faces. We hear that "symbols" of God must be inclusive to express all human experience, for they worship a god whom they have cast up from their own self-fulfilling experience, which in Scripture is called an idol. But, "you cannot drink the cup of the Lord and the cup of demons" (1 Cor. 10:21).

Such insincere practices as these are often perpetrated by church officials, with little or no sense of accountability to the ecclesial bodies they serve. There is much talk of the "community," but one also hears: "If the institutional church must die, so be it. It is for the sake of the gospel." Of course, what they mean by "the gospel" is the egalitarian ideology they serve, not the gospel of Jesus Christ. It appears also that there is a certain hardening setting in. Where these hypocrisies are exposed, the effort to defend their position becomes extreme.

The situation is particularly acute at many institutions of theological education, in which the egalitarian ideology often rages almost unchecked. Here one experiences the pedagogical tactics of theological fascism, only on the political left. I am personally aware of a case in which an instructor of theology in a mainline seminary dared to cross the line of critiquing liberation theology.

Upon criticizing liberation theology as a "twisting and distorting" of the gospel, the instructor was accused of "verbally assaulting" the students in the class. When reading from the King James Psalter as a devotional to begin class, he was accused of "mentally raping" the students. When expounding the Sermon on the Mount, in particular Jesus' command concerning divorce, and holding to the issue during a final exam, he was accused of "verbal abuse" of students. Based on the reports of "verbal abuse," prior to any investigation of the reports, he was asked—and declined—to resign from the seminary. He was told that a hearing would follow, and then later told that the hearing would not take place, "for his sake" and the sake of the seminary. Based on the report of "verbal abuse" and "mental rape" of the students, he was relieved of teaching the required course at the seminary, was dismissed from its ministry seminar, was eliminated from the roster for chapel. In the end, he was banned from all public teaching and stripped of all roles in the faculty governance of the seminary. All without any due process, without any public hearing.

This instructor was told by the dean of the faculty that it is "inappropriate" for a professor of systematic theology to expound Scripture in class. It was suggested that the instructor was a "fundamentalist," and upon presenting the same arguments from Calvin and Luther, he was told that it is not necessary to take Calvin and Luther so seriously. And this from an institution with a distinguished heritage grounded in the Reformation, in which the students are now told by an instructor in church history that, according to Luther, "the Bible never tells us how God is, only how we feel about God"!

These are examples from one case only; I have no doubt that other theological faculty could add to the list. The effect of such tactics is always to silence criticism, and in particular to shield it carefully from the public. Liberation theology, like liberalism before it, thrives on the subterfuge of concealing from the church at large its own defection from the gospel.

We must observe another of the fascist tactics of the liberation theologians. As we have seen, they hurl the epithet "fundamentalist!" at their opponents. What do they mean? Because they can "construe" language based on its "use" they can ignore history, and in a sense mean whatever they want to mean. Such, of course, is the typical tactic of ideology. What do they mean by fundamentalist? The older use of the term was to refer to one who located the offense of the gospel in the wrong place, drawing a line of essential doctrine where there isn't one. But countercultural liberalism has used the word to mean one who will not embrace "pluralism." This is more strange theological doublespeak for denial of the basic Christian confession that there is no salvation outside of Jesus Christ. If that is what is meant by fundamentalism, then there is not now, nor ever has been, a confessing Christian who is not a "fundamentalist." Augustine was a "fundamentalist"; Thomas was a "fundamentalist"; Calvin and Luther were "fundamentalists"; Wesley was a "fundamentalist"; confessing Lutherans are "fundamentalists"; confessing Baptists are "fundamentalists"; confessing Methodists are "fundamentalists"; confessing Episcopalians are "fundamentalists." This is nothing less than the gospel itself, the evangelical faith itself, which is being ridiculed, despised, and maligned. This is the evangelical faith for which men and women in the history of the church have given up their comfort, their honor, their reputation, their personal health and well-being, and at times even their lives. This is the evangelical faith for which we are called to leave everything, even our very lives, in order to come and follow Jesus Christ. If that is what the word "fundamentalist" is to mean, then let those who are not "fundamentalists" be exposed as wolves in the midst of the sheep. Let the people of God, who know Jesus Christ as the world's only hope, see to it that those who do not confess the one Lord and Savior are turned aside as imposters in the teaching office of the church.

Who indeed are the fundamentalists? Who operate with a handful of misinterpreted "proof-texts" from Scripture that are hauled out at every occasion to further "the cause"? Who are virtually unread in the literature of the history of theology, utterly unable to sustain serious theological debate concerning the great classics of the faith? Who are hiding their own obscurantist and negligent "learnings" in the tradition of the faith with appeals to "congregational studies" and "new models of religious education" and "contextualized immersion experiences" and the like? The effect of these, and other subterfuges, is to render themselves unaccountable to any authority outside themselves. As Calvin put it, "their will alone is *autopistos,* and all other reasons are bidden good-bye."

The evasions clearly go well beyond theological faculty at the seminaries. The ideology of egalitarianism has, in the short period of thirty years, sunk its roots deep into the institutional life of North American Christianity at every level. What once were learned societies for academic debate of theological and biblical scholarship have become virtual boot camps of ideological propaganda for liberation theology in one form or another. Whole foundations are devoting time and energy to the work of "faculty consensus," which is the euphemism for eliminating any opposition to liberation theology. At one such meeting, after a thinly disguised presentation on "postmodernism," the foundation speaker, in very ominous tones, declared, "Of course, we will never go back." He was referring to the days before the present ideology set in. His comments, and their tone, do bespeak a certain hardening among the liberation theologians and preachers that will perhaps only increase.

Do I exaggerate? The sad fact is that I have likely only scratched the surface. I have no doubt that other tactics have been used elsewhere, other insincere practices, other "teaching methods" deployed for the purposes of reinforcing the false doctrine. I am also aware of a similar debate surrounding so-called political correctness in North American culture. Even the "world" is more sincere and accountable than the liberation theologians!

By Their Fruits

We have argued that liberation theologians and preachers are false prophets of another gospel, wolves in the midst of the sheep of the Good Shepherd. We have argued on the basis of the false doctrine that they preach, substituting an egalitarian ideology for the gospel of Christ, and on the basis of the tactics that they employ, abusing the good order of Christ's church. Now we turn to another criterion in Holy Scripture: qualification for positions of leadership in the church of Jesus Christ.

Those who teach egalitarianism, who reject Christ's clear command to us concerning the different roles of men and women in marriage—wives are to be submissive to their husbands, husbands are to live considerately with their wives as "joint heirs of the grace of life" (1 Pet. 3:1–7)—are they not divorced? Are they not to be "above reproach, the husband of one wife"? Those who teach the "construal" of Scripture based on "community"; is the "community" they seek to "build" in the church to be the same as the divorce and adultery in their homes? "For if a man does not know how to manage his own household, how can he care for God's church?" (1 Tim. 3:5). It is, sadly, no surprise that their marriages should suffer. What lies at the bottom of the egalitarian ideology of liberation theology is nothing but the pseudogospel of self-fulfillment. It is no surprise that those who teach us "I am somebody!" should find it impossible to be faithful in marriage; that those who preach the "I feel" ideology should have little regard for the claim of Christ in our homes. "Partnership" is simply strange theological doubletalk for licentiousness and immorality. But what is shocking is the church's willingness to permit such teachers and preachers to manage its affairs. Much like with the televangelist scandals, even the "world" is suspicious of such behavior!

The civil rights movement, together with the theology of Karl Barth and others, unleashed on the church a virtual generation of false teaching. It is possible to look back now with deep regret at the havoc that was wreaked on the church, often by a few bad appointments, a few deeply unfortunate choices for leadership. "A little leaven leavens the whole lump." It is also possible to observe the fruits of the flesh that show up wherever false doctrine is taught, especially in the leaders of the ideology. It is, humanly speaking, clear that the heritage of many institutions in the church is seriously threatened, in some cases perhaps not to be remedied. How are we to respond?

God Is Our Refuge

The church of Jesus Christ has had its back against the wall before, surrounded by enemies within and without. God has not left us without a witness concerning his good will for our lives, and concerning our proper response of faith in the midst of trial.

God is our refuge and strength, a very present help in trouble.
Therefore will not we fear, though the earth be removed, and
  though the mountains be carried into the midst of the sea;
Though the waters thereof roar and be troubled, though the
  mountains shake with the swelling thereof. Selah.
There is a river, the streams whereof shall make glad the city
  of God, the holy place of the tabernacles of the most High.
God is in the midst of her; she shall not be moved: God shall
  help her, and that right early.
The heathen raged, the kingdoms were moved: he uttered
  his voice, the earth melted.
The Lord of hosts is with us; the God of Jacob is our refuge.
  Selah.
Come, behold the works of the Lord, what desolations he
  hath made in the earth.
He maketh wars to cease unto the end of the earth; he
  breaketh the bow, and cutteth the spear in sunder; he
  burneth the chariot in the fire.
Be still, and know that I am God: I will be exalted among the
  heathen, I will be exalted in the earth.
The Lord of Hosts is with us; the God of Jacob is our refuge.
  Selah.

—Psalm 46, KJV

Conclusion

> For by grace you have been saved through faith; and this is not your own doing, it is the gift of God—not because of works, lest any man should boast. For we are his workmanship, created in Christ Jesus for good works, which God prepared beforehand, that we should walk in them. (Eph. 2:8–10)

According to Scripture, we cannot understand the person and work of Jesus Christ unless we understand the person and work of the Holy Spirit. And we cannot understand the person and work of the Holy Spirit unless we understand the person and work of Jesus Christ. We come to understand both solely through the Word heard in faith, which is itself the means for the Lord's work.

"By grace you have been saved through faith." Our human condition was not one of the suffering of the innocent needing liberation, nor the morally weak needing empowerment for the sake of fulfilling the law of love. We were dead in our trespasses and sins. We were enslaved to sin, utterly unable to remedy our condition. We knew the Law, God's righteous claim upon our lives, but we could not do the Law, for sin worked in us death, bringing the curse of the Law. "We were by nature children of wrath, like the rest of mankind." Enslaved to our passions and desires, we were darkened in mind, haters of God and of one another, doing the works of evil. We stood guilty before a just and holy God.

But while we were yet sinners, Christ loved us and gave himself for us, the righteous for the unrighteous. We were not the innocent, in need of a liberator, but the guilty, in need of a Savior. Despite our sin, in the midst of our complete enslavement to sin and wickedness, God loved us—he did not despise or hate us, but loved us—and gave his Son as a sacrifice for our sins, to cover our guilt, to cancel the debt, to take God's just condemnation of us on his shoulders, in order to reconcile us to himself. God raised him from the dead, and highly exalted him above all things. Whoever believes in Jesus Christ, and in God who raised him from the dead, is forgiven.

Here we are not in partnership with God, for he did what we could not do. Here we are not fulfilling the command to love, for we were enslaved to sin, utterly unable to do what we knew was God's good will. Here we do not cooperate with God in any way whatsoever, for God alone has done everything for us, while we were dead in our sin. Here there is no free will, no human capacity; here there is only grace, here there is only the utterly free gift of God's amazing salvation. Here we are called to faith in Jesus Christ, not to works of the Law. Here faith itself is the instrument for receiving the free gift, the instrument that God himself supplies, while we were utterly dead in our trespasses and sins.

"For we are his workmanship, created in Christ Jesus for good works, which God prepared beforehand, that we should walk in them." We are not empowered by God; we who were dead in our sins, God made alive together with Christ. The Christian is not empowered but is a new creation in Jesus Christ. It is by the power of the Holy Spirit alone that we are set free from the law of sin and death by the blood of Jesus Christ, and raised to walk in new life in unity with the risen Lord. We are not empowered, but crucified with Christ; our flesh, our old nature, is not liberated but put to death. And we are not liberated, but created anew in Christ Jesus. The power is the Spirit's alone from beginning to end.

But what is the purpose of our new creation in Jesus Christ through the Holy Spirit dwelling within us? We are not created to "fulfill ourselves," but to be holy. The work of the Holy Spirit, in contrast to the work of the spirit of Antichrist, is the work of sanctification, the work of creating and transforming us into a holy people. The work of the Holy Spirit fashions us as God's people, not into a "community" of the masses, a mere crowd; the Holy Spirit works in each member of the body of Christ, through the personal faith of each Christian. We are to bear one another's burdens; but we know that each of us will have to bear his or her own load.

And what is the content of the good works that God has prepared for us beforehand? What is the new nature that Christ calls us to put on? In order to know what the liberation theologians do not know, our minds are to be transformed by the mercies of God, that we may discern God's good and perfect will. By the Spirit's work in us we understand that the will of God revealed in his Law is holy, just, and good; by the Spirit's work in us we come freely to desire, above all else, to do God's revealed will, to be consecrated, mind, body, and feelings, wholly and only unto him. By the Spirit's work in us we come to know that God's one eternal will is Jesus Christ himself, and that our sanctification is thus being conformed to his image, obeying his commandments, his revealed will in his Word, the Law of Christ.

To be a Christian means to be thus ruled by Jesus Christ himself through his Word and Spirit, by faith. To be a Christian means to walk in the Spirit, where "I" am not the ruler of my life ("I am somebody") but Jesus Christ himself, his living person, is the ruler of my life. To be a Christian means to bear the fruit of the Spirit, love, joy, and peace. That is what it means to inherit the kingdom of Christ, for which a person must be born again by the Spirit of God.

Nothing else counts for anything. What counts is a new creation. "Peace and mercy be upon all who walk by this rule, upon the Israel of God" (Gal. 6:16).

Select Bibliography

Classical Liberalism

Tillich, Paul. *Systematic Theology.* Chicago: University of Chicago Press, 1967.

Tracy, David. *Blessed Rage for Order: The New Pluralism in Theology.* New York: Seabury Press, 1975.

Liberation Theology

Brown, Robert McAfee. *Liberation Theology.* Louisville: Westminster/John Knox Press, 1993.

Cone, James. *The God of the Oppressed.* Minneapolis: Seabury Press, 1975.

Daly, Mary. *Beyond God the Father: Toward a Philosophy of Women's Liberation.* Boston: Beacon Press, 1973.

Gutiérrez, Gustavo. *A Theology of Liberation.* Maryknoll: Orbis Books, 1973.

Ruether, Rosemary. *Sexism and God-Talk.* Boston: Beacon Press, 1983.

Russell, Letty. *The Future of Partnership.* Philadelphia: Westminster Press, 1979.

Sobrino, Jon. *Christology at the Crossroads: A Latin American Approach.* Maryknoll: Orbis Books, 1978.

Thistlewaite, Susan Brooks, and Mary Potter Engel, eds. *Lift Every Voice.* San Francisco: Harper and Row, 1990.

West, Cornel. *Prophesy Deliverance! An Afro-American Revolutionary Christianity.* Philadelphia: Westminster Press, 1982.

Countercultural Liberalism

Barr, James. *Fundamentalism.* Philadelphia: Westminster Press, 1978.

Brueggemann, Walter. *Interpretation and Obedience.* Minneapolis: Fortress Press, 1991.

Frei, Hans W. *The Eclipse of Biblical Narrative.* New Haven and London: Yale University Press, 1974.

Hodgson, Peter C., and Robert H. King, eds. *Christian Theology: An Introduction to Its Traditions and Tasks.* 2d ed. Philadelphia: Fortress Press, 1985.

Kelsey, David. *The Uses of Scripture in Recent Theology.* Philadelphia: Fortress Press, 1975.

Lindbeck, George A. *The Nature of Doctrine.* Philadelphia: Westminster Press, 1984.

Moltmann, Jurgen. *The Way of Jesus Christ.* New York: HarperCollins, 1990.

Index

Barmen Declaration, 27–28, 47–48, 49, 80
Barth, Karl, 20–21, 27–30, 39–41, 48–49, 64–65, 72, 85
  biblical exegesis of, 29–30, 57–58
  Christology of, 28–29
  Biblical Theology of the Old and New Testaments, 54
Black church, witness of, 38, 71
Bonhoeffer, Dietrich, 50
Bundesgeschichte, 40, 57, 65

Calvin, John, 55, 83
Childs, Brevard, 54
Christian, definition of, 89
Christology, Barthian, 29–30
Church, the, 43–52
  as messianic community, 44–47
Church Dogmatics, 28, 29, 39, 40, 57, 64, 71
Civil rights movement, 19, 37, 45–46, 47, 71, 85
Cone, James, 18
Confession of the Presbyterian Church (1967), 27, 28, 48, 77
Construal, imaginative, 56–57
Contextualization, of Scripture, 55, 56
Cost of Discipleship, The, 50
Covenant, new, 42
Covenant-partnership, 17, 34, 36, 39–42, 65
Cross
  as stumbling block, 77
  as symbol, 74, 75

Daly, Mary, 18
Discipline, church, 79–80
Doctrine, false, 79–86
Doublespeak, theological, 24, 25, 28, 38, 62

Egalitarianism, 17, 25, 27–28, 44, 45, 48, 55, 67, 84, 85
Enlightenment ideology, 19, 32, 54
Evangelical Theology: An Introduction, 28
Evangelism, 44, 50
Evangelization, 44, 50
Exodus, the, mythology of, 34, 35, 36

Fascism, liberation theology as, 44, 45, 80–84
Faith, 69–77
Fides ex auditu, 30–31
"Fundamentalists," evangelical Christians as, 28, 41–42, 50, 52, 56, 82–83

Globalization, 71, 76
God, name of, 61–68
  dishonoring of, 64–67
  hallowing of, 61–62
Gospel, and Law, 49, 75
Guitiérrez, Gustavo, 18

Hermeneutical circle, 55–56
Historical-critical method, ideological use of, 26, 58
Hitler, Adolf, 45

Inclusive language, 62, 80

93